QUEST FOR BIBLE KNOWLEDGE

1,206 Trivia Questions to Sharpen Your Understanding of Scripture

EXCLUSIVELY UTILIZING THE KING JAMES VERSION OF THE OLD AND NEW TESTAMENTS

Handpicked by Trivia Expert & Nationally Syndicated Columnist

WILSON CASEY

T0348861

Good Books

New York, New York

Good Books books may be purchased in bulk at special discounts for sales promotion, corporate gifts, fund-raising, or educational purposes. Special editions can also be created to specifications. For details, contact the Special Sales Department, Good Books, 307 West 36th Street, 11th Floor, New York, NY 10018 or info@skyhorsepublishing.com.

Good Books in an imprint of Skyhorse Publishing, Inc.®, a Delaware corporation.

Visit our website at www.goodbooks.com.

10 9 8 7 6 5 4 3 2 1

Library of Congress Cataloging-in-Publication Data is available on file.

Cover design by David Ter-Avanesyan
Cover photo credit: Getty Images

Print ISBN: 978-1-68099-959-4
Ebook ISBN: 978-1-68099-960-0

Printed in the United States of America

*To my daughter, **Colleen Adaire Casey**,*
the possessor of great fortitude—you are
my heart.

Special Thanks

*Dr. **Phillip W. Holman** (Gaffney, South*
*Carolina) and **Mr. Buddy Pattillo***
(Spartanburg, South Carolina), as these two
gentlemen were my most diligent proofreaders.
(Gracious others listed in Acknowledgments.)

All scripture is given by inspiration of God, and is profitable for doctrine, for reproof, for correction, for instruction in righteousness.
—2 Timothy 3:16

If we ever forget that we're one nation under God, then we will be a nation gone under.
—Ronald Reagan

About this book, author, and inspiration . . .

Throughout the research and study, the author genuinely felt God's presence and divine guidance. Writing this book has been a profound and rewarding journey that demanded dedication, passion, and a commitment to delivering God's message through inspirational trivia the world needs.

The Bible's King James Version (KJV) was exclusively used for all content and research. Every book of the Old and New Testament is represented within this work of God's inspiration.

Out of respectful memory, the author used his late grandfather's Bible (W. Carl Lanford, b. 1886–d. 1976). It was my Pa-Pa's large-letter print edition. The author's mother, Helen L. Casey (b. 1910–d. 1980), taught him, "There's nothing more important than being in church on Sunday morning."

The author's reflective thoughts, "It'd be a much better world if all of us would realize—we're only here a very short time and just passing through, as this book's main purpose is to glorify God."

A special thanks to the two main formative churches in the author's life. Antioch Baptist Church in Enoree, South Carolina, where he was baptized as a twelve-year-old, and to Trinity United Methodist Church in Spartanburg, South Carolina, where he is a current active member.

Wilson Casey's goal: "I am hoping and praying that through my biblical trivia questions, readers will be divinely triggered to learn more about the Good Book and apply it to their daily lives. As together, with God's love, grace, and salvation, let's make this a better world for all."

Introduction:
A Wonderful Resource

Due to inspirational popularity, this is the follow-up to *Test Your Bible Knowledge,* which is still available. You now have in your hands *Quest for Bible Knowledge: 1,206 Trivia Questions to Sharpen Your Understanding of Scripture.* Having both works provides 2,412 challenging biblical multiple-choice questions with answers referenced in scripture. Each work is independent of each other, so having one version is great, but having both is phenomenal!

Paraphrasing the late humorist Will Rogers, "We're all ignorant, but only on different subjects." I, as the author of my **eighth** biblical trivia work, want to make you less ignorant about the Bible. Please note that there is absolutely nothing trivial about the Bible. The scriptures are God's holy words as written down by man (2 Timothy 3:16). This "trivia" work is intensified to reference, entertain, and solemnly educate. But that's not to say we all can't have a little fun learning along the way.

Think you know the Bible? Prove it by challenging yourself, your family, friends, bible study group, or class with the 1,206 more multiple-choice questions contained within to tantalize the intellect! These quizzes cover the entire scope of the Holy Bible, exclusively based on the beloved King James Version (KJV). As devised by a trivia world record holder (from a thirty-hour radio trivia marathon correctly identifying answers to 3,333 consecutive questions), these teasers are handpicked personal favorites. The correct answers include references to the relevant passages in scripture. There's also a self-scoring system with lines to jot down notes.

With questions devised to test your divine smarts, this work contains 201 separate quizzes with multiple-choice responses. Quizzes 1–194 run the random gamut of biblical appeal, while quizzes 195–201 are topical (Love, Evil, Labour, Liberty, Thanksgiving, Christmas, and Easter). Designed to teach, challenge, and enlighten, this collection of trivia guarantees hours of stimulating fun for all ages and knowledge levels. These informative questions surround the subject matter meaning the most in our lives.

This is a great book for Bible study. With each question posed you can look up the verses to gather the fuller story to which it pertains. This aspect is an empowering and rewarding experience to serve as a powerful base for building and continuing your biblical discipline. Bible trivia is everything a lover of the Lord could ask for, and is much, much more than just another quiz book in the marketplace. It's a reference guide with a handy index to trigger deeper study and understanding.

Respectfully, and may God bless, I'd love to hear from you. Feel free to email me and/or *please* support my Patreon web pages that provide six new general trivia questions every day, with Sundays always being biblical, plus plenty of bonus ones!

Wilson Casey
www.patreon.com/triviaguy
trivguy@bellsouth.net
Spartanburg, South Carolina

P.S. You'll really enjoy the ease of finding correct answers. They're on the same page with corresponding teasers posed. No thumbing to the back, nor flipping around losing your place.

Have Fun! Praise the Lord! And Pass the Trivia!

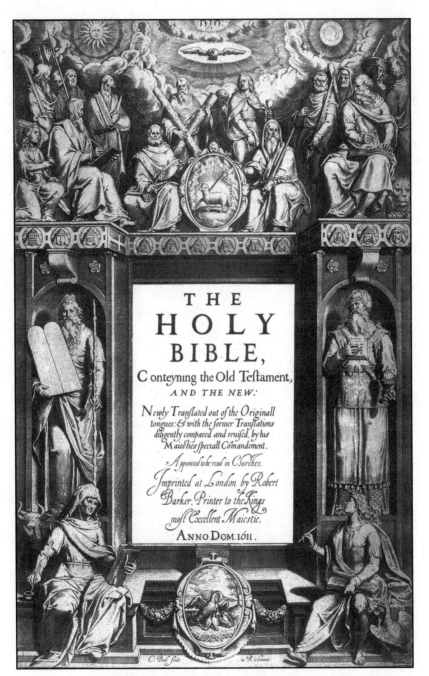

First Edition King James Version (KJV), 1611 A.D.
Courtesy of: Wikimedia Commons

Quiz 1

1. Is the book of Romans in the Old Testament, New Testament, or neither?
2. Some were known by more than one name; what was Thomas's other name?
   Andrew, Didymus, Caleb, Zimri
3. From Mark 5, who asked, "Who touched my clothes"?
   Jesus, John the Baptist, David, Solomon
4. In what body of water was Jesus baptized?
   Dead Sea, River Jordan, Sea of Galilee, River Cherith
5. From Hebrews 5, what Old Testament priest was Jesus like?
   Melchisedec, Eli, Josiah, Abihu
6. Which biblical name means "son of consolation"?
   Aaron, Barnabas, Gideon, Matthew

ANSWERS:

1. New (sixth book in the New Testament)
2. Didymus (John 11:16)
3. Jesus (Mark 5:30)
4. River Jordan (Matthew 3:13)
5. Melchisedec (Hebrews 5:6)
6. Barnabas (Acts 4:36)

Score Correct: _____ Date: _____ Name: _____
Study Notes: _____
_____
_____

Quiz 2

1. Is the book of Philesians in the Old Testament, New Testament, or neither?
2. What was the nationality of Goliath?
    Perizzite, Egyptian, Philistine, Cushite
3. At the end of Acts, where in Rome is Paul?
    Dungeon, King's palace, Temple, Hired house
4. In which book's ninth chapter does it mention the constellation Orion?
    Genesis, Exodus, Job, Jonah
5. From the gospel of John 1, what was "in the beginning"?
    The Earth, The Heavens, The Word, The Spirit
6. In the sight of the elders of Israel, where did Moses bring water out of a rock?
    Horeb, Carmel, Pisgah, Gilboa

ANSWERS:

1. Neither (Fictitious name combining Philippians and Ephesians)
2. Philistine (1 Samuel 17:4)
3. Hired house (Rented) (Acts 28:30)
4. Job (Job 9:8–9)
5. The Word (John 1:1)
6. Horeb (Exodus 17:6)

Score Correct: _____ Date: _____ Name: _____
Study Notes: _____
_____
_____

Quiz 3

1. Is the book of Jonah in the Old Testament, New Testament, or neither?
2. What did Sarah say she had not been doing, therefore lying to God?
   Walking, Eating, Laughing, Lusting
3. From the book of Ecclesiastes, there is "a time to be born, and a time to . . ."?
   Live, Eat, Die, Praise
4. Where does the Bible say, "One Lord, one faith, one baptism"?
   John 3:16, Ephesians 4:5, Romans 11:12, Daniel: 7:9
5. The Lord will have war with whom from generation to generation?
   Hesbolah, Eliezer, Amalek, Pilate
6. Abigail, Michal, and Ahinoam were all wives of . . . ?
   Solomon, Peter, Obadiah, David

ANSWERS:

1. Old (Thirty-second book in the Old Testament)
2. Laughing (Genesis 18:13–15)
3. Die (Ecclesiastes 3:2)
4. Ephesians 4:5
5. Amalek (Exodus 17:16)
6. David (1 Samuel 25:42–44)

Score Correct: _____ Date: _____ Name: _____
Study Notes: _____
_____
_____

Quiz 4

1. Is the book of Capernaum in the Old Testament, New Testament, or neither?
2. In the book of Acts, who recounts the story of Abraham along with the captivity and freedom of the children of Israel?
   Paul, Peter, Stephen, Andrew
3. The Lord saith, "thoughts of peace, and not of _____, to give you an expected end."
   Harm, Evil, Malice, Demons
4. From 1 Kings 6, who constructed the first altar covered with gold?
   Gideon, Josiah, Noah, Solomon
5. Who went to sleep and fell out the window while Paul preached?
   Esua, Enid, Eutychus, Eucyrus
6. In what Macedonian city were Paul and Silas imprisoned?
   Philippi, Neapolis, Jericho, Jerusalem

ANSWERS:
1. Neither (Galilean city on the western shore)
2. Stephen (Acts 7)
3. Evil (Jeremiah 29:11)
4. Solomon (1 Kings 6:21)
5. Eutychus (Acts 20:7–12)
6. Philippi (Acts 16:12)

Score Correct: _____ Date: _____ Name: _____
Study Notes: _____
_____
_____

Quiz 5

1. Is the book of Obadiah in the Old Testament, New Testament, or neither?
2. Who escaped to Zoar upon hearing wicked cities were going to be destroyed?
   Gomorrah, Elijah, Lot, Shimei
3. Who confessed to an angel after beating his mule that he had sinned?
   Sodom, Balaam, Samuel, Daniel
4. From Job 4, who was so frightened by a dream that his hair stood on end?
   Eliphaz, Abraham, Ehud, Joseph
5. Who had to parade his eight sons before a prophet as found in 1 Samuel?
   Aaron, Jacob, Naboth, Jesse
6. From Exodus 14, whose chariots were lost in the Red Sea?
   Solomon's, Pharaoh's, Samson's, Ahab's

ANSWERS:
1. Old (Thirty-first book of the Old Testament)
2. Lot (Genesis 19:18–23)
3. Balaam (Numbers 22:23–35)
4. Eliphaz (Job 4:1, 15)
5. Jesse (1 Samuel 16:8–13)
6. Pharaoh's (Exodus 14:26–28)

Score Correct: _____ Date: _____ Name: _____
Study Notes: _____
_____
_____

Quiz 6

1. Is the book of Lucius in the Old Testament, New Testament, or neither?
2. Which member of David's army murdered two generals and was slain at a tabernacle altar as punishment?
   Heliz, Elika, Joab, Zalmon
3. From Acts 28, who was bitten on the hand by a snake, as he laid sticks on a fire?
   Noah, Moses, David, Paul
4. What prophet did mouth-to-mouth on a dead boy, thus restoring him to life?
   Jonathan, Silas, Elisha, Nahash
5. From Genesis 21, who put her child under a bush to die?
   Hagar, Miriam, Ezra, Sarah
6. What grandmother got commended by Paul for her great faith?
   Rachel, Lois, Dorcas, Delilah

ANSWERS:

1. Neither (Lucius of Cyrene was a teacher in Antioch)
2. Joab (1 Kings 2:28–34)
3. Paul (Acts 28:3)
4. Elisha (2 Kings 4:32–35)
5. Hagar (Genesis 21:14–16)
6. Lois (2 Timothy 1:4–6)

Score Correct: _____ Date: _____ Name: _____
Study Notes: _____
_____
_____

Quiz 7

1. Is the book of Concubines in the Old Testament, New Testament, or neither?
2. From Daniel 4, who had the vision of a tree growing higher and higher until it could be seen by everyone?
   Silas, Josiah, Nebuchadnezzar, Solomon
3. Which book could be summarized, "God, why don't you stop bad things from happening"?
   Habakkuk, Zephaniah, Haggai, Malachi
4. What hour mentioned in the Bible means the last possible moment something can be done?
   1st, 3rd, 11th, 12th
5. Which king of Israel set up two golden calves as gods, one in Bethel, the other in Dan?
   Zimri, Jeroboam, Baasha, Ahaziah
6. From Judges 6, where did Gideon encounter an angel in Ophrah?
   Prison, Under an oak tree, Temple, Well

ANSWERS:

1. Neither (Females conjugally united to a man, but relations inferior to that of a wife)
2. Nebuchadnezzar (Daniel 4:4–5, 11)
3. Habakkuk (Writer's words are addressed to God)
4. 11th (Matthew 20:6–9)
5. Jeroboam (1 Kings 12: 28–33)
6. Under an oak tree (Judges 6:11–12)

Score Correct: _____ Date: _____ Name: _____
Study Notes: _____
_____
_____

Quiz 8

1. Is the book of Galatians in the Old Testament, New Testament, or neither?
2. What's the one kind of woman a priest cannot marry?
   Harlot, Divorcee, Heathen, Virgin
3. Who was grateful for a gourd that shaded his head, thus delivering him from misery?
   Bartimaeus, Zophar, Moses, Jonah
4. In Matthew. what did Jesus say would not prevail against His church?
   Gates of hell, Lust, Evil forces, Satan's army
5. Whom did God smite for taking hold of the Ark of the Covenant?
   Nathan, Hiram, Samuel, Uzzah
6. What was the forbidden fruit Adam and Eve ate?
   Not specified, Pear, Apple, Fig

ANSWERS:

1. New (Ninth book of the New Testament)
2. Divorcee (her that is put away) (Ezekiel 44:21–22)
3. Jonah (Jonah 4:6–7)
4. Gates of hell (Matthew 16:18)
5. Uzzah (2 Samuel 6:6–7)
6. Not specified (Genesis 3:6)

Score Correct: _____ Date: _____ Name: _____
Study Notes: _____
_____
_____

Quiz 9

1. Is the book of Kanah in the Old Testament, New Testament, or neither?
2. From Exodus law, what's the penalty to whoever smiteth his father or mother?
    Death, Starved, Stoned, Blinded
3. Called Artemis in some translations, who was the goddess of Asia who had a temple in Ephesus?
    Dagon, Hermes, Diana, Baal
4. From the book of Matthew, who referred to believers as "salt of the earth"?
    Jesus, John, Mark, Paul
5. Whose was the voice of one crying in the wilderness?
    Eli, Aaron, Samuel, John the Baptist
6. From John 3, what did Jesus compare the power of the Spirit to?
    Sea, Wind, Mountains, Masses

ANSWERS:

1. Neither (Stream forming the boundary between Ephraim and Manasseh)
2. Death (Exodus 21:15)
3. Diana (Acts 19:26–27)
4. Jesus (Matthew 5:1, 13)
5. John the Baptist (Matthew 3:1–3)
6. Wind (John 3:8)

Score Correct: _____ Date: _____ Name: _____
Study Notes: _____
_____
_____

Quiz 10

1. Is the book of Levite in the Old Testament, New Testament, or neither?
2. Where did Jesus stay when John the Baptist was in prison?
   Beersheba, Capernaum, Assos, Cana
3. What king slew the Gibeonites, breaking his promise of peace and angering God?
   Neco, Joash, Jehu, Saul
4. In 1 Corinthians what "churches of" worshipped on the first day of the week?
   Adventist, Galatia, Gideon, Balaam
5. Whose wife's mother lay sick of a fever and was healed by Jesus?
   Mark, Judas, Simon, Joel
6. From Proverbs 22, "A good name is rather to be chosen than great . . ."?
   Riches, Witness, Corruption, Love

ANSWERS:
1. Neither (A member of the tribe of Levi)
2. Capernaum (Matthew 4:12–13)
3. Saul (2 Samuel 21:1–2)
4. Galatia (1 Corinthians 16:1–2)
5. Simon (Mark 1:30–31)
6. Riches (Proverbs 22:1)

Score Correct: _____ Date: _____ Name: _____
Study Notes: _____
_____
_____

Quiz 11

1. Is the book of Uzzi in the Old Testament, New Testament, or neither?
2. What did Jesus say a man could forfeit, negating the gain of the whole world?
   Life, Love, House, Soul
3. Though Eunice and the apostle Paul were not married, they both called whom their son?
   Timothy, Barnabas, Didymus, Mark
4. How many years will Jesus reign on earth before Satan's final judgment?
   7, 50, 1000, 5000
5. Who was known as the "father of all who play the harp and organ"?
   Solomon, Jubal, David, Jeremiah
6. In Genesis 2 what watered the Garden of Eden?
   Rain, Sea, River, Angel

ANSWERS:

1. Neither (Son of Bukki and father of Zerahiah)
2. Soul (Mark 8:36)
3. Timothy (2 Timothy 1:1–5)
4. 1000 (Revelation 20:6–10)
5. Jubal (Genesis 4:21)
6. River (Genesis 2:10)

Score Correct: _____ Date: _____ Name: _____
Study Notes: _____
_____
_____

Quiz 12

1. Is the book of Mandrake in the Old Testament, New Testament, or neither?
2. How did Jesus instruct Judas to do his evil of betrayal?
   Abundantly, Quickly, Insincerely, Peacefully
3. The book of Hebrews tells us to entertain strangers, as they may be . . . ?
   Demons, Angels, Prophets, Reincarnated
4. The river that watered the Garden of Eden divided into how many heads?
   2, 4, Dozens, Hundreds
5. From Genesis 2, who/what named the animals?
   God, Serpent, Adam, Eve
6. The first five books of the Bible are called the books of . . . ?
   Moses, Adam, Noah, Cain

ANSWERS:

1. Neither (Plant generally associated with its supposed power of granting fertility)
2. Quickly (John 13:27)
3. Angels (Hebrews 13:2)
4. 4 (Genesis 2:10–14)
5. Adam (Genesis 2:19–20)
6. Moses (In secondary title of each book)

Score Correct: _____ Date: _____ Name: _____
Study Notes: _____
_____
_____

Quiz 13

1. Is the book of Aaron in the Old Testament, New Testament, or neither?
2. Jesus said, "That whosoever believeth in me should not abide in . . ."?
   Fear, Darkness, Shame, Sin
3. Where was Samson imprisoned after being betrayed by Delilah?
   Bethany, Antioch, Gaza, Damascus
4. From 1 Peter 2, what types of stones were built into a spiritual house?
   Lively, Rolling, Precious, River
5. From Genesis 17, what was the name of Abraham's wife?
   Ruth, Anna, Abigail, Sarah
6. From the book of Genesis, who was Sarah's Egyptian handmaid?
   Adah, Esther, Matred, Hagar

ANSWERS:

1. Neither (Eldest son of Amram and Jochebed, and first anointed priest)
2. Darkness (John 12:46)
3. Gaza (Judges 16:1–3, 21)
4. Lively (1 Peter 2:5)
5. Sarah (Genesis 17:15)
6. Hagar (Genesis 16:1)

Score Correct: _____ Date: _____ Name: _____
Study Notes: _____
_____
_____

Quiz 14

1. Is the book of Jacob in the Old Testament, New Testament, or neither?
2. From Genesis 41, who had the vision (dream) of seven fat cows coming out of a river?
    Adam, Moses, Pharaoh, Abraham
3. Where was Jesus crucified?
    Samaria, Colossae, Golgotha, Gethsemane
4. Which prophet's word caused Syrian soldiers to be struck blind?
    Gad, Jubal, Solomon, Elisha
5. Absalom ordered his servants to set whose barley crops on fire?
    Job, Joab, Jethro, Jehoshabeath
6. What church did John describe as one with an "open door"?
    Sardis, Philadelphia, Antioch, Smyrna

ANSWERS:

1. Neither (Second born of the twin sons of Isaac by Rebekah)
2. Pharaoh (Genesis 41:1–2)
3. Golgotha (Mark 15:22–24)
4. Elisha (2 Kings 6:8, 18)
5. Joab (2 Samuel 14:29–31)
6. Philadelphia (Revelation 3:7–8)

Score Correct: _____ Date: _____ Name: _____
Study Notes: _____
_____
_____

Quiz 15

1. Is the book of Behemoth in the Old Testament, New Testament, or neither?
2. In Genesis 28, who had the vision of angels going up and down a ladder reaching into Heaven?
   Joseph, Ahab, Ehud, Jacob
3. Which Psalm begins, "The Lord is my shepherd, I shall not want"?
   1, 11, 23, 50
4. From Acts 10, where did Cornelius encounter an angel?
   Temple, Well, House, Field
5. The name Barnabas being interpreted means the son of . . . ?
   The Field, Fasting, Consolation, Tempest
6. Who were the two sisters of Lazarus, Mary and. . . ?
   Ruth, Martha, Sarah, Miriam

ANSWERS:
1. Neither (Translated as beast or cattle)
2. Jacob (Genesis 28:10–12)
3. 23 (Psalms 23)
4. House (Acts 10:1–3)
5. Consolation (Acts 4:36)
6. Martha (John 11:1–2)

Score Correct: _____ Date: _____ Name: _____
Study Notes: _____
_____
_____

Quiz 16

1. Is the book of Genesis in the Old Testament, New Testament, or neither?
2. From 2 Samuel, what king confessed his adulterous affair after being confronted by the prophet Nathan?
   Silas, Josiah, Jael, David
3. In Acts 19, where were books worth fifty thousand silver coins burned at a public bonfire?
   Gezer, Samaria, Ephesus, Jericho
4. From Genesis 29, what childless woman was jealous of her sister's fertility?
   Candace, Abigail, Rachel, Herodias
5. How many years old was Ahaziah when he began his reign in Jerusalem?
   7, 42, 68, 90
6. What famous prophet was the son of Amoz?
   Paul, Isaiah, Peter, John the Baptist

ANSWERS:

1. Old (First book of Old Testament)
2. David (2 Samuel 12:7–9)
3. Ephesus (Acts19:17–19)
4. Rachel (Genesis 30:1)
5. 42 (2 Chronicles 22:2)
6. Isaiah (2 Kings 19:2)

Score Correct: _____ Date: _____ Name: _____
Study Notes: _____
_____
_____

Quiz 17

1. Is the book of Song of Solomon in the Old Testament, New Testament, or neither?
2. Whose son, Mahershalalhashbaz, is the longest human name in the Bible?
   Judas, Enoch, Isaiah, Abednego
3. From John 13, who said to Jesus, "Thou shalt never wash my feet"?
   Paul, Peter, Andrew, Thomas
4. When Paul addressed the Athenians, what did some of them mock?
   Virgin birth, Resurrection, Great flood, Good Samaritan
5. In Acts 9, what woman had Tabitha as a pet name?
   Priscilla, Naomi, Dorcas, Delilah
6. Which church was neither hot nor cold?
   Antioch, Laodicea, Trinity, Philadelphia

ANSWERS:

1. Old (Twenty-second book of Old Testament)
2. Isaiah (Isaiah 8:1–3)
3. Peter (John 13:8)
4. Resurrection (Acts 17:21, 32)
5. Dorcas (Acts 9:36)
6. Laodicea (Revelation 3:14–16)

Score Correct: _____ Date: _____ Name: _____
Study Notes: _____
_____
_____

Quiz 18

1. Is the book of Zillah in the Old Testament, New Testament, or neither?
2. Who saw a vision of a woman called Wickedness flown away in a basket by two angels?
   Jonathan, Dodo, Zechariah, Belshazzar
3. From Judges 17, who confessed to his mother about stolen pieces of silver?
   David, Micah, Jonah, Esau
4. In Genesis 3, who/what guards the Garden of Eden?
   Roaring lions, Armed angels, Golden rams, God Himself
5. How many psalms in the book of Psalms are attributed to Moses?
   1, 5, 34, 74
6. In the Bible, how many men are named "Dodo"?
   1, 2, 3, 4

ANSWERS:

1. Neither (One of the wives of Lamech)
2. Zechariah (Zechariah 5:8–9)
3. Micah (Judges 17:1–2)
4. Armed angels (Genesis 3:24)
5. 1 (Psalm 90)
6. 3 (Judges 10:1, 2 Samuel 23:9, 24)

Score Correct: _____ Date: _____ Name: _____
Study Notes: _____
_____
_____

Quiz 19

1. Is the book of Job in the Old Testament, New Testament, or neither?
2. From Luke 15, the woman who searched her house with a lantern was looking for a lost what?
   Soul, Child, Bird, Silver coin
3. As mentioned in Exodus, from what ailment/disease was Moses healed?
   Slurred speech, Leprosy, Roaring fever, Multiple seizures
4. Whose hairs were grown like eagles' feathers, and his nails like birds' claws?
   Daniel, Matthew, Luke, Nebuchadnezzar
5. What was the most frequent name Jesus called himself?
   Son of Man, Lamb of God, Bread of Life, Son of God
6. What was the Hebrew name of Paul?
   Simon Peter, Andrew, Haggai, Saul

ANSWERS:

1. Old (Eighteenth book of Old Testament)
2. Silver coin (Luke 15:8–9)
3. Leprosy (Exodus 4:6–7)
4. Nebuchadnezzar (Daniel 4:33)
5. Son of Man (around eighty-one times)
6. Saul (Acts 13:9)

Score Correct: _____ Date: _____ Name: _____
Study Notes: _____
_____
_____

Quiz 20

1. Is the book of Vashti in the Old Testament, New Testament, or neither?
2. Located at a plain in the land of Shinar, how far up was the Tower of Babel supposed to reach?
   Top of mountains, Unto heaven, Beyond the stars, Above the trees
3. Who, of Jabin's army, had 900 iron chariots and made twenty years of life unbearable for the Israelites?
   Tobiah, Pilate, Sisera, Absalom
4. How old was Abram when Hagar bore their son, Ishmael?
   25, 86, 100, 162
5. Who paid Delilah to betray the mighty Samson?
   The Pharaoh, Abdi, Lords of the Philistines, Jeuz
6. In which city were eighty-five priests slain?
   Gezer, Nob, Shechem, Aphek

ANSWERS:

1. Neither (Queen of King Ahasuerus)
2. Unto heaven (Genesis 11:2–4, 9)
3. Sisera (Judges 4:2–3)
4. 86 (Genesis 16:16)
5. Lords of the Philistines (Judges 16:4–5)
6. Nob (1 Samuel 22:18–19)

Score Correct: _____ Date: _____ Name: _____
Study Notes: _____
_____
_____

Building the Tower of Babel
Courtesy of: clipart.christiansunite.com

Quiz 21

1. Is the book of 2 Samuel in the Old Testament, New Testament, or neither?
2. How many pieces of silver did Joseph's brothers get when they sold him into slavery?
   0, 2, 19, 20
3. Where does it command brides to shave their heads and manicure their nails?
   Exodus, Leviticus, Numbers, Deuteronomy
4. From Genesis 27, to whom did Isaac give a blessing?
   Jacob, Abraham, Moses, Noah
5. Who said to God, "What wilt thou give me, seeing I go childless"?
   Abram, Samson, Solomon, Aaron
6. From 1 Kings, which prophet was fed by birds?
   Paul, David, Elisha, Elijah

ANSWERS:

1. Old (Tenth book of Old Testament)
2. 20 (Genesis 37:27–28)
3. Deuteronomy (21:12)
4. Jacob (Genesis 27:22–29)
5. Abram (Genesis 15:2)
6. Elijah (1 Kings 17:1, 4–6)

Score Correct: _____ Date: _____ Name: _____
Study Notes: _____
_____
_____

Quiz 22

1. Is the book of Zaphnath in the Old Testament, New Testament, or neither?
2. Along with a goat and heifer, which is not among the animals God asked Abram to bring him as a sacrifice?
   Ram, Turtledove, Pigeon, Viper
3. Who honored a man by letting him ride the royal steed through city streets?
   Silas, Hosea, Ahasuerus, Asa
4. From Acts 9, what dressmaker was restored to life by Peter's prayers?
   Dorcas, Leah, Jezebel, Miriam
5. Pharaoh gave what burnt city to his daughter for a gift?
   Cana, Gezer, Joppa, Bethel
6. Who called Herod an adulterer in Mark 6?
   Samson, John the Baptist, Jacob, Zimri

ANSWERS:

1. Neither (First part of Joseph's name called by Pharaoh, Zaphnathpaaneah)
2. Viper (Genesis 15:2, 9)
3. Ahasuerus (Esther 6:2, 7–11)
4. Dorcas (Acts 9:36–42)
5. Gezer (1 Kings 9:16)
6. John the Baptist, (Mark 6:17–18)

Score Correct: _____ Date: _____ Name: _____
Study Notes: _____
_____
_____

Quiz 23

1. Is the book of Tyre in the Old Testament, New Testament, or neither?
2. What is easier to go through a needle's eye, than for a rich man to enter into the kingdom of God?
   Firestick, Ox, Sandal, Camel
3. During a famine, who told another man they should set out to find grass to feed their horses and mules?
   Abishag, Ahab, Abner, Agrippa
4. What are epistles, as described in 2 Corinthians?
   Apostles, Temples, Letters, Flocks
5. Who died on a mountaintop after being garment stripped by Moses?
   Eleazar, Abraham, Noah, Aaron
6. How many times does the word "eternity" occur in the Bible?
   0, 1, 74, 212

ANSWERS:

1. Neither (Ancient Phoenician city twenty miles south of Sidon on today's coast of Lebanon)
2. Camel (Luke 18:25)
3. Ahab (1 Kings 18:2, 5–6)
4. Letters (2 Corinthians 3:1)
5. Aaron (Numbers 20:28)
6. 1 (Isaiah 57:15)

Score Correct: _____ Date: _____ Name: _____
Study Notes: _____
_____
_____

Quiz 24

1. Is the book of 1 John in the Old Testament, New Testament, or neither?
2. Who did the chief priests plot to kill because his resurrection caused many to believe in Jesus's power?
   Lazarus, Eutychus, Elisha, Zarephath
3. Along with honeycomb, what type of fish did Jesus eat after His resurrection?
   Boiled, Raw, Broiled, Fried
4. How old was Joshua, Moses's successor, when he died?
   110, 187, 210, 312
5. What did the sick people at Gennesaret touch of Jesus to be healed?
   His feet, Border (fringe) of garment, His hands, Staff
6. How many times is the word "paradise" mentioned in the scriptures?
   1, 3, 5, 7

ANSWERS:

1. New (Twenty-third book of New Testament)
2. Lazarus (John 12: 9–11)
3. Broiled (Luke 24:41–43)
4. 110 (Joshua 24:29)
5. Border (fringe) of garment (Mark 6:53–56)
6. 3 (Luke 23:43, 2 Corinthians 12:4, Revelation 2:7)

Score Correct: _____ Date: _____ Name: _____
Study Notes: _____
_____
_____

Quiz 25

1. Is the book of Ezekiel in the Old Testament, New Testament, or neither?
2. Fill in the blank from the Lord's Prayer, "Our Father which art in heaven, hallowed be thy _____."
   Word, Love, Name, Salvation
3. Which of these cities was destroyed by brimstone and fire from the Lord out of heaven?
   Jericho, Haran, Paphos, Sodom
4. In Luke 2, who recognized the child Jesus when He was brought to the Temple?
   Barnabas, Simeon, Pope Linus, Stephen
5. What did Adam call his wife's name, because she was the mother of all living?
   Ruth, Naomi, Eve, Esther
6. How many stones did David take with him to fight Goliath?
   2, 5, 7, 14

ANSWERS:

1. Old (Twenty-sixth book of Old Testament)
2. Name (Matthew 6:9, Luke 11:2)
3. Sodom (Genesis 19:24–25)
4. Simeon (Luke 2:25–28)
5. Eve (Genesis 3:20)
6. 5 (1 Samuel 17:39–40)

Score Correct: _____ Date: _____ Name: _____
Study Notes: _____
_____
_____

Quiz 26

1. Is the book of Achish in the Old Testament, New Testament, or neither?
2. What said unto Balaam, "What have I done unto thee, that thou hast smitten me these three times"?
   Camel, Dog, Ass (donkey), Ram
3. From Matthew 17, Peter was told he would find what with a piece of money in its mouth?
   Ram, Fish, Viper, Raven
4. What man of little stature climbed a sycamore tree to see Jesus pass?
   Zeboim, Zacchaeus, Zebudah, Zebul
5. Reuben was Jacob's firstborn and one of the sons of whom?
   Sarah, Rebecca, Rachel, Leah
6. Paul was born in Tarsus, a city in . . . ?
   Thessalonica, Phrygia, Cilicia, Ur

ANSWERS:

1. Neither (King of the Philistine city of Gath)
2. Ass (donkey) (Numbers 22:28)
3. Fish (Matthew 17:24–27)
4. Zacchaeus (Luke 19:2–5)
5. Leah (Genesis 35:23)
6. Cilicia (Acts 21:39)

Score Correct: _____ Date: _____ Name: _____
Study Notes: _____
_____
_____

Quiz 27

1. Is the book of Zechariah in the Old Testament, New Testament, or neither?
2. What bird released from Noah's Ark served as a first attempt to discover dry land?
    Raven, Pigeon, Sparrow, Hawk
3. Who were the Israelites fighting on the day when the sun stood still?
    Philistines, Midianites, Amorites, Gibeonites
4. Which book referred to Jesus as "The Prince of Peace"?
    Matthew, Mark, Ezekiel, Isaiah
5. From Joshua 2, who hid two spies on a roof?
    Hosea, Ezra, Rachel, Rahab
6. How many stories were in Noah's Ark?
    1, 2, 3, 4

ANSWERS:

1. Old (Thirty-eighth book of Old Testament)
2. Raven (Genesis 8:5–7)
3. Amorites (Joshua 10:12–13)
4. Isaiah (Isaish 9:6)
5. Rahab (Joshua 2:3–6)
6. 3 (Genesis 6:16)

Score Correct: _____ Date: _____ Name: _____
Study Notes: _____
_____
_____

Quiz 28

1. Is the book of Nephilim in the Old Testament, New Testament, or neither?
2. Who ended many of his letters, "Grace be with you"?
   John the Baptist, Paul, John the Revelator, Jude
3. What repulsive creatures bit the Israelites in the wilderness?
   Scorpions, Fiery serpents, Vipers, Ravens
4. Jesus said that we should seek, knock, and do what?
   Adorn, Ask, Try, Inspire
5. Who did God choose to replace Moses to lead the Israelites?
   Aaron, Jacob, Joshua, Caleb
6. Which Psalm is the longest of all Psalms?
   23, 110, 119, 150

ANSWERS:

1. Neither (Beings described as large and strong)
2. Paul (Colossians 4:18, 2 Timothy 4:22, Titus 3:15)
3. Fiery serpents (Numbers 21:6)
4. Ask (Matthew 7:7)
5. Joshua (Joshua 1:1–2)
6. 119 (22 stanzas with 176 verses)

Score Correct: _____ Date: _____ Name: _____
Study Notes: _____
_____
_____

Quiz 29

1. Is the book of Salome in the Old Testament, New Testament, or neither?
2. According to Paul, who must be blameless, the husband of one wife, vigilant, sober, and of good behavior?
   Bishop, Butler, Scribe, Potter
3. "In every nation he that feareth him, and worketh righteousness, is _____ with him."
   Righteous, Accepted, Obedient, Trustworthy
4. People who say that Jesus is not from God are controlled by the spirit of the . . . ?
   Damned, Antichrist, Weakened, Beguiled
5. What color was the thread Rahab bound in her window?
   Black, Purple, Green, Scarlet
6. Jesus was descended from what Old Testament king?
   David, Jehoash, Baasha, Nadab

ANSWERS:
1. Neither (Wife of Zebedee and Hebrew greeting of peace)
2. Bishop (1 Timothy 3:2)
3. Accepted (Acts 10:35)
4. Antichrist (1 John 4:3)
5. Scarlet (Joshua 2:3, 18)
6. David (Matthew 1:19–20)

Score Correct: _____ Date: _____ Name: _____
Study Notes: _____
_____
_____

Quiz 30

1. Is the book of 1 Kings in the Old Testament, New Testament, or neither?
2. What tree did Jesus tell a parable about in that God is true and certain?
   Apple, Fig, Olive, Cedar
3. "Let everything that hath breath praise the Lord" is found in what book?
   Psalms, Proverbs, Numbers, Jeremiah
4. What did Abel, the second son of Adam and Eve, do for a living?
   Carpenter, Keeper of sheep, Farmer, Tentmaker
5. Who was the father of John the Baptist?
   Zechariah, Zacharias, Zephaniah, Zaccheus
6. Which of these is *not* a book of the New Testament?
   Revelation, Judges, Colossians, Jude

ANSWERS:

1. Old (Eleventh book of Old Testament)
2. Fig (Luke 21:29–33)
3. Psalms (Psalms 150:6)
4. Keeper of sheep (Genesis 4:1–2)
5. Zacharias (Luke 1:13, 67)
6. Judges (Seventh book of Old Testament)

Score Correct: _____ Date: _____ Name: _____
Study Notes: _____
_____
_____

Quiz 31

1. Is the book of Irad in the Old Testament, New Testament, or neither?
2. From Proverbs 29, "But whoso putteth his trust in the Lord shall be . . ."?
   Made whole, Blessed, Safe, Wise
3. Upon which mountaintop did Balaam instruct Balak to build seven altars?
   Olives, Sinai, Peor, Carmel
4. What does God want us to keep as the apple of our eye?
   His law, Brotherly love, Faithfulness, Righteousness
5. What did David do to Goliath once he slew him?
   Stole his armor, Robbed him, Cut off his head, Buried him
6. In scripture, who was the first woman judge in Israel?
   Deborah, Sarah, Jezebel, Lydia

ANSWERS:

1. Neither (Son of Enoch and grandson of Cain)
2. Safe (Proverbs 29:25)
3. Peor (Numbers 23:28–29)
4. His law (Proverbs 7:2)
5. Cut off his head (1 Samuel 17:51)
6. Deborah (Judges 4:4)

Score Correct: _____ Date: _____ Name: _____
Study Notes: _____

_____
_____

Quiz 32

1. Is the book of Meshach in the Old Testament, New Testament, or neither?
2. Which bodily part of his twin brother Esau was Jacob holding onto when he came out of the womb?
   Hand, Elbow, Heel, Knee
3. What minor prophet was first a shepherd among the herdsmen of Tekoa?
   Hosea, Joel, Amos, Obadiah
4. To whom did Jesus say, "Get thee behind me, Satan"?
   Andrew, Rizpah, Elijah, Peter
5. Who prayed three times a day at an open window?
   Daniel, Jonah, Stephen, Solomon
6. What was Abraham's original name?
   Aaron, Jared, Enoch, Abram

ANSWERS:
1. Neither (One of the men thrown into a fiery furnace by Nebuchadnezzar II)
2. Heel (Genesis 25:24–26)
3. Amos (Amos 1:1)
4. Peter (Matthew 16:23)
5. Daniel (Daniel 6:10)
6. Abram (Genesis 17:5)

Score Correct: _____ Date: _____ Name: _____
Study Notes: _____
_____
_____

Quiz 33

1. Is the book of Lahairoi in the Old Testament, New Testament, or neither?
2. Which Psalm begins, "O God, thou art my God; early will I seek thee"?
   60, 63, 74, 117
3. From Proverbs 22, what is foolishness bound in the heart of?
   Wicked, Poor, Child, Foolish
4. Who led the Israelites over the River Jordan?
   Moses, Joshua, Aaron, Elijah
5. What was the name of Samson's father?
   Noah, Manoah, Jesse, Levi
6. The book of Proverbs was primarily written by?
   Jude, Moses, Solomon, Isaac

ANSWERS:

1. Neither (A well near Kadesh)
2. 63 (Psalms 63)
3. Child (Proverbs 22:15)
4. Joshua (Joshua 3:1)
5. Manoah (Judges 13:22–24)
6. Solomon (Proverbs 1:1, most scholars agree)

Score Correct: _____ Date: _____ Name: _____

Study Notes: _____

_____

_____

Quiz 34

1. Is the book of Patrobas in the Old Testament, New Testament, or neither?
2. Who said, "Lo, I dwell in a house of cedars but the ark of the covenant . . . remaineth under curtains"?
   David, Nathan, Saul, Solomon
3. Why was Miriam shut out of camp for seven days?
   Ungodly act, Leprous, Fasting, Lent
4. Who took David in as his own after the slaying of Goliath?
   Jonathan, Solomon, Saul, Eliakim
5. Jesus said, "For with God all things are _____."
   Righteous, Forthcoming, Pure, Possible
6. David was around how many years old when he died?
   15, 44, 70, 102

ANSWERS:
1. Neither (A Christian in Rome to whom Paul sent greetings)
2. David (1 Chronicles 17:1)
3. Leprous (Numbers 12:10–15)
4. Saul (1 Samuel 17:57, 18:1–2)
5. Possible (Mark 10:27)
6. 70 (2 Samuel 5:4, 1 Kings 2:10–11)

Score Correct: _____ Date: _____ Name: _____
Study Notes: _____
_____
_____

Quiz 35

1. Is the book of Neapolis in the Old Testament, New Testament, or neither?
2. Which apostle raised Tabitha, who by interpretation was called Dorcas, from the dead?
    Philip, Peter, Matthew, Thomas
3. The Ethiopian eunuch that Philip met was under what queen?
    Azubah, Candace, Nehushta, Vashti
4. At whose well did Jesus meet the Samaritan woman?
    Joshua's, Jonah's, Jacob's, Judas's
5. Who was king during Zechariah's time of prophecy?
    David, Daniel, Darius, Saul
6. How long did Aaron's followers mourn him?
    3 days, 13 days, 30 days, 3 months

ANSWERS:

1. Neither (A seaport of Macedonia)
2. Peter (Acts 9:36–37, 40–41)
3. Candace (Acts 8:26–27)
4. Jacob's (John 4:6–7)
5. Darius (Zechariah 1:7)
6. 30 days (Numbers 20:29)

Score Correct: _____ Date: _____ Name: _____
Study Notes: _____
_____
_____

Quiz 36

1. Is the book of Lebanon in the Old Testament, New Testament, or neither?
2. Saith the Lord of hosts, "I am jealous for Jerusalem and for _____"?
   Mankind, Zion, Israel, Nazareth
3. From Proverbs, what happens when the wicked have authority?
   People mourn, Heavens blacken, Masses kill, Taxes abound
4. "Blessed are the meek, for they shall _____."
   Obtain mercy, Inherit the earth, See God, Be called children of God
5. In which book does one find the Good Samaritan parable?
   Matthew, Mark, Luke, John
6. From Numbers, what animal did God allow to speak?
   Lamb, Ass (Donkey), Camel, Ram

ANSWERS:

1. Neither (Country in the Levant region of West Asia)
2. Zion (Zechariah 1:14)
3. People mourn (Proverbs 29:2)
4. Inherit the earth (Matthew 5:5)
5. Luke (Luke 10:25–37)
6. Ass (Donkey) (Numbers 22:28–30)

Score Correct: _____ Date: _____ Name: _____
Study Notes: _____

_____

_____

Quiz 37

1. Is the book of Malachi in the Old Testament, New Testament, or neither?
2. After Moses had written down the book of the law, where did he tell the people to store it?
    Levite tent, Behind river rocks, Mountaintop, Beside the Ark of the Covenant
3. How did David go up by the ascent of Mount Olivet (Olives)?
    Dancing and yelling, Barefoot and weeping, Singing and skipping, Crying and praying
4. In 1 Kings 20, who besieged and made war against Samaria after gathering his forces?
    Benhadad, Menahem, Rezin, Omri
5. What king asked for the help of a woman who was a medium?
    Jehu, Amaziah, Saul, Neco
6. By what other name was Gideon known?
    Jerubbaal, Jairus, Jehizkiah, Jehoash

ANSWERS:

1. Old (Thirty-ninth and last book of the Old Testament)
2. Beside the Ark of the Covenant (Deuteronomy 31:24–26)
3. Barefoot and weeping (2 Samuel 15:30)
4. Benhadad (1 Kings 20:1)
5. Saul (1 Samuel 28:7)
6. Jerubbaal (Judges 8:35)

Score Correct: _____ Date: _____ Name: _____
Study Notes: _____
_____
_____

Quiz 38

1. Is the book of Boaz in the Old Testament, New Testament, or neither?
2. What was the site for Moses's burial place, in a valley in the land of Moab, over against . . . ?
   Paphos, Bethpeor, Petra, Bethshan
3. Who said, "Thou art Peter, and upon this rock I will build my church"?
   Jesus, Aaron, Mark, Joseph
4. Which king was referred to by Jesus as "that fox"?
   Herod, Solomon, Ahab, Caesar
5. Who said, "Be sure your sin will find you out"?
   Matthew, David, Noah, Moses
6. Who was the firstborn son of Jacob?
   Aaron, Joseph, Reuben, Simeon

ANSWERS:

1. Neither (Wealthy landowner of Bethlehem in Judea)
2. Bethpeor (Deuteronomy 34:5–6)
3. Jesus (Matthew 16:18)
4. Herod (Luke 13:31–32)
5. Moses (Numbers 32:20–23)
6. Reuben (Genesis 35:23)

Score Correct: _____ Date: _____ Name: _____
Study Notes: _____
_____
_____

Quiz 39

1. Is the book of Mark in the Old Testament, New Testament, or neither?
2. The first verse of which book is "The elder unto the well-beloved Gaius, whom I love in the truth"?
   1 Samuel, 1 Chronicles, 2 Peter, 3 John
3. From Exodus 25, what pure gold cover was placed on the Ark of the Covenant?
   Mercy seat, Mordecai lid, Mina top, Myrrha mirror
4. Which prophet was famous for his vision of the dry bones?
   Hosea, Ezekiel, Jeremiah, Nathan
5. Who was a seller of purple goods from Thyatira?
   Lamara, Lala, Ledah, Lydia
6. Whose sisters were Zeruiah and Abigail?
   David, Ishbaal, Eleazar, Solomon

ANSWERS:

1. New (Second book of the New Testament)
2. 3 John (3 John 1:1)
3. Mercy seat (Exodus 25:16–17)
4. Ezekiel (Ezekiel 37:3–5)
5. Lydia (Acts 16:14)
6. David (1 Chronicles 2:15–16)

Score Correct: _____ Date: _____ Name: _____
Study Notes: _____
_____
_____

Quiz 40

1. Is the book of Kandake in the Old Testament, New Testament, or neither?
2. Whose thigh went out of joint wrestling with a man (angel) until the breaking of the day?
   Adam, Moses, Jacob, Lot
3. When Jesus healed ten lepers, how many came back to thank Him?
   0, 1, 5, All 10
4. The pool of Bethesda is near which market in the city of Jerusalem?
   Sheep, Camel, Horse, Food
5. Who was Caiaphas's father-in-law?
   Annanias, Annas, Pilate, Nicodemus
6. What part of Leah was tender (weak)?
   Ears, Mind, Eyes, Voice

ANSWERS:
1. Neither (Ancient Ethiopian title given to queens)
2. Jacob (Genesis 32: 24–25)
3. 1 (Luke 17:12–15)
4. Sheep (John 5:2)
5. Annas (John 18:13)
6. Eyes (Genesis 29:17)

Score Correct: _____ Date: _____ Name: _____
Study Notes: _____
_____
_____

Jesus healing the ten lepers
Courtesy of: clipart.christiansunite.com

Quiz 41

1. Is the book of Menorah in the Old Testament, New Testament, or neither?
2. With whom did Lot escape the city of Sodom before it rained down brimstone and fire?
   Wife, Son, Two daughters, Three friends
3. Who tried to buy the Holy Spirit after he saw people receiving it from the apostles?
   Stephen, Timothy, Caiaphas, Simon
4. With what did the Israelites think God could not furnish them in the wilderness?
   Chair, Lamp, Table, Axe
5. Who was thrown from a window and struck the ground dead?
   Hezekiah, Jezebel, Joash, Abner
6. From 2 Peter, what should be added to one's faith?
   Church attendance, Virtue, Witnessing, Tithing

ANSWERS:

1. Neither (Seven-branched candelabrum and symbol representing the Jewish people)
2. Two daughters (Genesis 19:28–30)
3. Simon (Acts 8:18–20)
4. Table (Psalms 78:19)
5. Jezebel (2 Kings 9:30–33)
6. Virtue (2 Peter 1:5)

Score Correct: _____ Date: _____ Name: _____
Study Notes: _____
_____
_____

Quiz 42

1. Is the book of Philippians in the Old Testament, New Testament, or neither?
2. What was the minimum age regarding the rule for the Levites to be able to serve in the tabernacle?
   12, 16, 25, 30
3. The first chapter of which book begins, "Then Moab rebelled against Israel after the death of Ahab"?
   Exodus, 2 Kings, Job, Proverbs
4. Christ not only took on him the nature of angels, but the seed of whom?
   Abraham, Isaac, Ezekiel, Adam
5. Revelation is the last book of the Bible, with which being next-to-last?
   Joel, Hebrews, Jude, John
6. Where did Abram go after leaving Ur?
   Iconium, Nineveh, Haran, Salem

ANSWERS:
1. New (Eleventh book of the New Testament)
2. 25 (Numbers 8:22–24)
3. 2 Kings (2 Kings 1:1)
4. Abraham (Hebrews 2:16)
5. Jude (Twenty-sixth book of New Testament)
6. Haran (Genesis 11:31)

Score Correct: _____ Date: _____ Name: _____
Study Notes: _____
_____
_____

Quiz 43

1. Is the book of Necho in the Old Testament, New Testament, or neither?
2. Which herb, spice, or seasoning is mentioned most often in the Bible?
   Salt, Pepper, Sage, Thyme
3. Who said to Jesus Christ, "Thou art the Christ, the Son of the living God"?
   Thomas, John the Baptist, Simon Peter, Samaritan leper
4. God stretcheth out the north over the empty place, and hangeth the earth upon?
   Stars, Father's house, Nothing, Paradis
5. The first chapter of which book begins, "The former treatise have I made, O Theophilus"?
   Matthew, Luke, John, Acts
6. Which was good and found in Eden?
   Sapphires, Rubies, Diamonds, Gold

ANSWERS:

1. Neither (An Egyptian king)
2. Salt (At least thirty-five times)
3. Simon Peter (Matthew 16:15–17)
4. Nothing (Job 26:7)
5. Acts (Acts 1:1)
6. Gold (Genesis 2:10–12)

Score Correct: _____ Date: _____ Name: _____
Study Notes: _____
_____
_____

Quiz 44

1. Is the book of Dumah in the Old Testament, New Testament, or neither?
2. Who said, "It is not meet [right] to take the children's bread, and to cast it to dogs"?
   Jesus, Judas, Joshua, Jacob
3. How many times does the word "reverend" appear in the scriptures?
   0, 1, 6, 12
4. Where were Saul (Paul) and Barnabas deserted by Mark (called John)?
   Jericho, Perga, Athens, Damascus
5. Who was the treasurer that Isaiah was to see?
   Shebna, Sheerah, Shelomith, Samanntha
6. Whose sons were Jeuz, Shachia, and Mirma?
   Jesse, Shaharaim, Jethro, Gaal

ANSWERS:

1. Neither (Sixth son of Ishmael and grandson of Abraham and Hagar)
2. Jesus (Matthew 15:26)
3. 1 (Psalms 111:9)
4. Perga (Acts 13:7, 13)
5. Shebna (Isaiah 22:15)
6. Shaharaim (1 Chronicles 8:8–10)

Score Correct: _____ Date: _____ Name: _____
Study Notes: _____
_____
_____

Quiz 45

1. Is the book of Ephesians in the Old Testament, New Testament, or neither?
2. The first chapter of whose book begins, "Now it came to pass in the thirtieth year, in the fourth month"?
   Ezra, Ezekiel, Micah, Malachi
3. What city was the site of Jacob's famous dream (Jacob's ladder)?
   Lachish, Perga, Haran, Bethel
4. Who/what did the Lord choose for his peculiar treasure?
   Fig tree, Israel, Job, Water
5. How many children did Hannah have?
   5, 10, 15, 20
6. Of which of these creatures did the prophet Joel have a vision?
   Flies, Locust, Vipers, Leeches

ANSWERS:
1. New (Tenth book of the New Testament)
2. Ezekiel (Ezekiel 1:1)
3. Bethel (Genesis 28:12, 18)
4. Israel (Psalms 135:4)
5. 5 (1 Samuel 2:21)
6. Locust (Joel 1:1–4)

Score Correct: _____ Date: _____ Name: _____
Study Notes: _____
_____
_____

Quiz 46

1. Is the book of Cormorant in the Old Testament, New Testament, or neither?
2. The first chapter of which book begins, "Paul, an apostle of Jesus Christ by the commandment of God"?
   1 Timothy, Titus, James, 2 John
3. Who killed a giant that had on every hand six fingers and on every foot six toes?
   Mephibosheth, Jambres, Abimelech, Jonathan
4. What fell from Saul's eyes when he regained his sight, something like . . . ?
   Ants, Scales, Blood, Salt
5. From 1 Kings 6, who built the first temple in Jerusalem?
   Samuel, Joshua, Solomon, Aaron
6. What Roman soldier was led to Christ by Peter?
   Cornelius, Dan, Menahem, Felix

ANSWERS:
1. Neither (A bird forbidden as food, similar to a pelican)
2. 1 Timothy (1 Timothy 1:1)
3. Jonathan (2 Samuel 21:20–21)
4. Scales (Acts 9:17–18)
5. Solomon (1 Kings 6:1–2)
6. Cornelius (Acts 10:1–5)

Score Correct: _____ Date: _____ Name: _____
Study Notes: _____
_____
_____

Quiz 47

1. Is the book of Jubilee in the Old Testament, New Testament, or neither?
2. Why had Jonah been thrown overboard from a ship, later to be swallowed by the big fish?
   He asked to, For stealing, Being a stowaway, Brandishing his sword
3. In Revelation, upon which river did the sixth angel pour out his vial?
   Euphrates, Blood, Gihon, Hiddekel
4. What "things of" does the natural man not receive?
   Heart, Spirit of God, Life, Righteous few
5. Who burned his son alive as a heathen sacrifice?
   Joab, Ahaz, Isaac, Josiah
6. Who stole images (idols) from her father?
   Elisabeth, Martha, Rachel, Deborah

ANSWERS:
1. Neither (Time of celebration and rejoicing)
2. He asked to (Jonah 1:7, 11–12)
3. Euphrates (Revelation 16:12)
4. Spirit of God (1 Corinthians 2:14)
5. Ahaz (2 Kings 16:2–4)
6. Rachel (Genesis 31:19)

Score Correct: _____ Date: _____ Name: _____
Study Notes: _____
_____
_____

Quiz 48

1. Is the book of Laodicea in the Old Testament, New Testament, or neither?
2. While Samson slept upon Deliah's knees who cut his hair, thus taking his strength away?
   Servant girl, Delilah, Unnamed man, Rebekah
3. 2 Kings 19 and which other book's chapter are almost alike word for word?
   Deuteronomy 7, Isaiah 37, Jeremiah 50, Job 16
4. What righteous man started the practice of herding sheep?
   Adam, Cain, Abel, Job
5. In biblical times, which was a large unit of money or weight?
   Levy, Talent, Shekel, Sepulcher
6. What was the reason Job's eye was dim?
   Dirt, Needle, Sweat, Sorrow

ANSWERS:

1. Neither (One of Seven Churches of Revelation, aka the Seven Churches of the Apocalypse)
2. Unnamed man (Judges 16:18–19)
3. Isaiah 37 (And 2 Kings 19)
4. Abel (Genesis 4:2, Hebrews 11:4)
5. Talent (Exodus 25:39, 2 Chronicles 25:6)
6. Sorrow (Job 17:7)

Score Correct: _____ Date: _____ Name: _____
Study Notes: _____
_____
_____

Quiz 49

1. Is the book of Luke in the Old Testament, New Testament, or neither?
2. Who did Abraham's servant give jewels of silver, and jewels of gold, and raiment?
   Esther, Mary Magdalene, Rebekah, Martha
3. In Genesis 6, how many years did God set as mankind's age limit?
   120, 490, 612, 969
4. Where does one go to find balm according to Jeremiah?
   Corinth, Joppa, Derbe, Gilead
5. Who tested the will of the Lord with a wool fleece?
   Jehu, Gideon, Amos, Ahaziah
6. With what did Mary Magdalene wipe Jesus's feet?
   Finest lace, Tablecloth, Her hair, Oils

ANSWERS:

1. New (Third book of New Testament)
2. Rebekah (Genesis 24:52–53)
3. 120 (Genesis 6:3)
4. Gilead (Jeremiah 46:11)
5. Gideon (Judges 6:36–40)
6. Her hair (John 12:3)

Score Correct: _____ Date: _____ Name: _____
Study Notes: _____
_____
_____

Quiz 50

1. Is the book of Leviathan in the Old Testament, New Testament, or neither?
2. King Saul is wounded in battle and perishes how?
   Stuck down by armor-bearer, Poisoned, Fell on own sword, Hanged by enemies
3. From the Old Testament, who was Abigail's first husband?
   Elimelech, Nabal, Aquila, Boaz
4. In the book of Revelation Jesus said, "I am Alpha and ..."?
   Beta, Omega, Eternity, Delta
5. From the book of Proverbs, what is held up as an example to the sluggard (lazy) man?
   Bee, Flea, Locust, Ant
6. How many sons did Jacob have?
   2, 4, 8, 12

ANSWERS:

1. Neither (Crooked serpent, possibly a crocodile)
2. Fell on own sword (1 Samuel 31:4)
3. Nabal (1 Samuel 25:3)
4. Omega (Revelation 22:13)
5. Ant (Proverbs 6:6)
6. 12 (Genesis 35:22)

Score Correct: _____ Date: _____ Name: _____
Study Notes: _____

_____

_____

Quiz 51

1. Is the book of Claudius in the Old Testament, New Testament, or neither?
2. Jesus said, "For what shall it _____ a man, if he shall gain the whole world, and lose his own soul"?
   Cherish, Profit, Worship, Leave
3. From John 10, to what type of animals are Christians compared?
   Camels, Sheep, Lions, Serpents
4. Whose life was saved when his wife put an image (idol) into his bed?
   Samson, David, Amon, Cyrus
5. From where did Jesus come to be baptized?
   Bashan, Galilee, Ephesus, Hebron
6. Who was Jacob and Leah's daughter?
   Dinah, Anna, Abigail, Candace

ANSWERS:

1. Neither (Roman emperor from 41–54 AD)
2. Profit (Mark 8:36)
3. Sheep (John 10:27–28)
4. David (1 Samuel 19:11–13)
5. Galilee (Matthew 3:13)
6. Dinah (Genesis 30:16, 21)

Score Correct: _____ Date: _____ Name: _____
Study Notes: _____
_____
_____

Quiz 52

1. Is the book of Goshen in the Old Testament, New Testament, or neither?
2. Who prophesied, "Therefore the Lord himself shall give you a sign; Behold, a virgin shall conceive, and bear a son"?
   John the Baptist, Zechariah, Isaiah, Andrew
3. What agricultural routine allowed the underprivileged, the poor, and strangers to obtain food?
   Harrowing, Agrarianism, Gleaning, Hard-panning
4. From Psalms, on referring to enemies, their throat is an open . . . ?
   Wound, Door, Sepulchre, Cave
5. Who was the king of Persia that God charged to build a temple?
   Darius, Artaxerxes, Cyrus, Cambyses
6. From Joel, what shall all faces gather?
   Sunlight, Blackness, Fear, Warmth

ANSWERS:

1. Neither (Region of ancient Egypt east of Nile Delta)
2. Isaiah (Isaiah 7:14)
3. Gleaning (Leviticus 19:9–10)
4. Sepulchre (Psalms 5:9)
5. Cyrus (Ezra 1:2)
6. Blackness (Joel 2:6)

Score Correct: _____ Date: _____ Name: _____
Study Notes: _____
_____
_____

Quiz 53

1. Is the book of 2 Kings in the Old Testament, New Testament, or neither?
2. Along with Stephen, Philip, Prochorus, Nicanor, Timon, and Parmenas, who's among the "Seven," often known as the "Seven Deacons"?
   Pedaiah, Mishael, Nicolas, Malchiah
3. While dreaming, where did Paul visualize a man standing who was asking him to come over and help?
   Ephesus, Caesarea, Antioch, Macedonia
4. If a man also lie with mankind, as he lieth with a woman, both of them have committed an?
   Abomination, Abhorrence, Obscenity, Atrocity
5. As a scribe, who was the first person to use a pulpit?
   Shavsha, Jehoshaphat, Baruch, Ezra
6. What type of wood did Noah utilize for building the ark?
   Cedar, Gopher, Carob, Olive

ANSWERS:

1. Old (Twelfth book of the Old Testament)
2. Nicolas (Acts 6:5)
3. Macedonia (Acts 16:9)
4. Abomination (Leviticus 20:13)
5. Ezra (Nehemiah 8:4)
6. Gopher (Genesis 6:13–14)

Score Correct: _____ Date: _____ Name: _____
Study Notes: _____
_____
_____

Quiz 54

1. Is the book of Reuel in the Old Testament, New Testament, or neither?
2. From Leviticus, a man or woman that is a "what" shall surely be put to death?
   Magician, Idol worshipper, Wizard, Gossiper
3. What sickly messenger visited Paul in prison?
   Marcus, Epaphroditus, Aristarchus, Demas
4. Who was the last prophet of the Old Testament?
   Hosea, Elijah, Micah, Malachi
5. What was the first-mentioned pulpit made of?
   Wood, Stone, Sand, Clay
6. Who first preached Christ unto the city of Samaria?
   Urijah, Shema, Philip, Anaiah

ANSWERS:

1. Neither (A son of Esau and Bashemath)
2. Wizard (Leviticus 20:27)
3. Epaphroditus (Philemon 1:9, Philippians 2:25–27)
4. Malachi (Last book of Old Testament)
5. Wood (Nehemiah 8:4)
6. Philip (Acts 8:4–5)

Score Correct: _____ Date: _____ Name: _____
Study Notes: _____
_____
_____

Quiz 55

1. Is the book of Ephesus in the Old Testament, New Testament, or neither?
2. When the disciples argued about who would be the greatest among them, who/what did Jesus set by Him?
   Lamb, Birds, Lilies, Child
3. What was the act of God in making the heavens and the earth and bringing forth life?
   Confirmation, Calvary, Creation, Communion
4. What was the relationship of Aquila and Priscilla who traveled with Paul?
   Brother and sister, Neighbors, Married couple, Uncle and aunt
5. What soothed the evil spirit that plagued Saul?
   Water, Animal sacrifices, Fire, Harp music
6. How many books of the Bible begin with the letter G?
   1, 2, 3, 4

ANSWERS:
1. Neither (City frequented by the apostle Paul, one of the Seven Churches of Revelation)
2. Child (Luke 9:46–48)
3. Creation (Mark 10:6, 13:9, Romans 1:20)
4. Married couple (Acts 18:2, 18:18)
5. Harp music (1 Samuel 16:15–17)
6. 2 (Genesis, Galatians)

Score Correct: _____ Date: _____ Name: _____
Study Notes: _____
_____
_____

Quiz 56

1. Is the book of Crete in the Old Testament, New Testament, or neither?
2. What word or phrase meaning "be opened" did Jesus say when he healed a deaf man?
   Codex sinaiticus, Ephphatha, Lama sabachthani, Talitha
3. All believers are called to be part of a royal. . .?
   Family, Priesthood, Flock, Wedding
4. What judge of Israel was a prostitute's son and made a captain?
   Hosea, Jephthah, Samson, Lot
5. In Revelation, how is Satan depicted?
   Silver goat, Black horse, Red dragon, 7-winged bat
6. What king did Esther eventually marry?
   Jehu, Omri, Ahasuerus, Zedekiah

ANSWERS:

1. Neither (Large Greek island)
2. Ephphatha (Mark 7:32–35)
3. Priesthood (1 Peter 2:7–9)
4. Jephthah (Judges 11:1, 11)
5. Red dragon (Revelation 12:3, 9)
6. Ahasuerus (Esther 2:16–17)

Score Correct: _____ Date: _____ Name: _____
Study Notes: _____
_____
_____

Quiz 57

1. Is the book of Mash in the Old Testament, New Testament, or neither?
2. When the blind man looked up after being healed by Jesus at Bethsaida, what did the men he saw look like?
   Giants, Sheep, Trees, Horses
3. From Ruth 1, who called herself Mara, a name meaning "bitter"?
   Priscilla, Miriam, Naomi, Deborah
4. Where did Samuel grow up serving the Lord in the tabernacle?
   Shiloh, Zeboim, Kirioth, Shechem
5. What set Jacob's flocks apart from those of Laban?
   Solid black, Speckled and spotted, All female, Sickly and dying
6. At what age was Joshua, the son of Nun, when he died?
   110, 162, 187, 202

ANSWERS:

1. Neither (One of the four sons of Aram)
2. Trees (Mark 8:22–24)
3. Naomi (Ruth 1:20)
4. Shiloh (1 Samuel 1:24)
5. Speckled and spotted (Genesis 30:27, 31–32)
6. 110 (Joshua 24:29)

Score Correct: _____ Date: _____ Name: _____
Study Notes: _____
_____
_____

Quiz 58

1. Is the book of Trinity in the Old Testament, New Testament, or neither?
2. When the Pharisees questioned and tempted Jesus seeking a sign from heaven, what sign did He give?
   No sign, Look to the sea, Mighty wind, 7 thunders
3. The Law of Moses stated that males should be circumcised how many days after they are born?
   3, 7, 8, 10
4. After hearing many things, what did Job call the ones after they tried to console him?
   Sore losers, Miserable comforters, Wretched sons, Cowardly lions
5. From Hebrews, what is the new veil we walk through for redemption?
   Sacrifices of money, Flesh of Christ, Blood of saviour, Love of God
6. What prophet was the son of Elkanah and Hannah?
   Samuel, Huldah, Daniel, Nathan

ANSWERS:

1. Neither (Doctrine of the unity of God as subsisting in three distinct Persons)
2. No sign (Mark 8:11–12)
3. 8 (Leviticus 12:1–3)
4. Miserable comforters (Job 16:2)
5. Flesh of Christ (Hebrews 10:20)
6. Samuel (1 Samuel 1:8, 20)

Score Correct: _____ Date: _____ Name: _____
Study Notes: _____
_____
_____

Quiz 59

1. Is the book of 2 John in the Old Testament, New Testament, or neither?
2. How did Paul have to address the Corinthians as they were not able to understand more than spiritual basics?
   As pagans, Babes in Christ, As soldiers, As wounded
3. Ezra arrived during what amount of time in his journey from Babylon to Jerusalem, in the . . . ?
   Seventh day, Third week, Fifth month, Second year
4. Who, perhaps, did Jesus give a standing ovation to in Acts?
   Herod, James, John the Baptist, Stephen
5. Jesus compared Christians to salt and . . . ?
   Water, Bread, Light, Mountains
6. Who's the runaway slave in the book of Philemon?
   Lemuel, Marcus, Doulos, Onesimus

ANSWERS:
1. New (Twenty-fourth book of the New Testament)
2. Babes in Christ (1 Corinthians 3:1)
3. Fifth month (Ezra 7:6–8)
4. Stephen (Acts 7:55–59)
5. Light (Matthew 5:13–14)
6. Onesimus (Philemon 1:9–17)

Score Correct: _____ Date: _____ Name: _____
Study Notes: _____
_____
_____

Quiz 60

1. Is the book of Daberath in the Old Testament, New Testament, or neither?
2. In which book does Jesus predict children rebelling against their parents to be a sign of end times?
   Matthew, Mark, Luke, John
3. How many days and nights did Jesus fast before his temptation by Satan?
   3, 12, 40, 7 x 70
4. From 1 Corinthians, who gives a spiritual increase?
   Labour bearers, Disciples, God, Angels
5. Who played the matchmaker for Isaac and Rebekah?
   Nahor, A shepherd, Bethuel, Abraham's servant
6. Job's children were killed due to a . . . ?
   Flood, Fire, Great wind, Stampede

ANSWERS:

1. Neither (A town of Issachar)
2. Mark (Mark13:7–8, 12)
3. 40 (Matthew 4:1–3)
4. God (1 Corinthians 3:6–7)
5. Abraham's servant (Genesis 24:52, 59, 66–67)
6. Great wind (Job 1:18–19)

Score Correct: _____ Date: _____ Name: _____
Study Notes: _____
_____
_____

Temptation of Jesus by Satan
Courtesy of: clipart.christiansunite.com

Quiz 61

1. Is the book of Ecclesiastes in the Old Testament, New Testament, or neither?
2. Which two, after offering strange fire before the Lord, suffered a devouring fire death from the Lord?
   James and Jude, Shem and Ham, Nadab and Abihu, Nahor and Haran
3. From the Law of Moses, how long was a woman considered unclean after she gave birth to a male?
   3 days, 7 days, 2 weeks, 4 weeks
4. Who had a vision of a man with a measuring line in his hand to measure Jerusalem?
   Zechariah, Daniel, Jacob, Solomon
5. For Paul knew nothing by himself, who did he say judged him?
   The Lord, Syrians, Gentiles, Pharisees
6. Who was an officer and captain of Pharaoh's guard?
   Medjay, Potiphar, Anubis, Sphinx

ANSWERS:

1. Old (Twenty-first book of the Old Testament)
2. Nadab and Abihu (Leviticus 10:1–2)
3. 7 days (Leviticus 12:1–2)
4. Zechariah (Zechariah 2:1–2)
5. The Lord (1 Corinthians 4:4)
6. Potiphar (Genesis 37:36, 39:1)

Score Correct: _____ Date: _____ Name: _____
Study Notes: _____
_____
_____

Quiz 62

1. Is the book of Zarqa in the Old Testament, New Testament, or neither?
2. To what city was Saul traveling when suddenly there shined around him a light from heaven?
   Jerusalem, Damascus, Anab, Ekron
3. How many days did it take Nehemiah to get the wall around Jerusalem completed?
   6, 52, 100, 1000
4. At what church was Paul accused of turning the world upside down?
   Antioch, Smyrna, Thessalonica, Galatia
5. In Genesis, the snake is supposed to strike at (bruise) what part of man?
   Throat, Hand, Heel, Eyes
6. Which book follows 2 Corinthians?
   1 Thessalonians, James, Galatians, Titus

ANSWERS:

1. Neither (Second largest tributary of the lower Jordan River)
2. Damascus (Acts 9:3, 8)
3. 52 (Nehemiah 6:15)
4. Thessalonica (Acts 17:1, 6)
5. Heel (Genesis 3:14–15)
6. Galatians (Ninth book of the New Testament)

Score Correct: _____ Date: _____ Name: _____
Study Notes: _____
_____
_____

Quiz 63

1. Is the book of Tiberias in the Old Testament, New Testament, or neither?
2. When Moses encountered the burning bush, what did the Lord instruct him to take off?
   Shoes, Cloak, Hat, Belt
3. From Hebrews, what, besides the ministry, are faithful ones urged to do?
   Tithe regularly, Resist evil, Gather together, Show compassion
4. How did Joash raise and get enough money to repair the temple?
   Sold all possessions, Raided royal treasury, Taxed the people, Neighboring king assisted
5. What does one have to become temporarily to become wise?
   Poor, Rich, Shepherd, Fool
6. How many days was Jesus on earth after His resurrection?
   3, 40, 100, 346

ANSWERS:

1. Neither (City on western shore of Sea of Tiberias)
2. Shoes (Exodus 3:2–5)
3. Gather together (Hebrews 10:22–25)
4. Taxed the people (2 Chronicles 24:4–6, 11–14)
5. Fool (1 Corinthians 3:18)
6. 40 (Acts 1:2–3)

Score Correct: _____ Date: _____ Name: _____
Study Notes: _____
_____
_____

Quiz 64

1. Is the book of Abednego in the Old Testament, New Testament, or neither?
2. In Hebrews, "By faith _____ was translated that he should not see death; and was not found, because God had translated him."
   Elijah, Enoch, Eber, Eleasah
3. By night, the Lord led the Israelites out of Egypt in a pillar of fire, and by day, in a pillar of . . . ?
   A cloud, Smoke, Sunshine, Rain
4. The shortest Psalm, 117, that centers around "Praise the Lord," has how many verses?
   2, 3, 4, 5
5. Over what brook was the Garden of Gethsemane located?
   Ophir, Cedron, Arnon, Besor
6. Who said his people should be holy because he is holy?
   Moses, The Lord, Abraham, Paul

ANSWERS:

1. Neither (One of the men thrown into a fiery furnace by Nebuchadnezzar II)
2. Enoch (Hebrews 11:5)
3. A cloud (Exodus 3:8, 13:21)
4. 2 (Psalms 117:1–2)
5. Cedron (Matthew 26:36, John 18:1). Called Kidron in Old Testament
6. The Lord (Leviticus 20:26)

Score Correct: _____ Date: _____ Name: _____
Study Notes: _____
_____
_____

Quiz 65

1. Is the book of Micah in the Old Testament, New Testament, or neither?
2. According to scripture, if you resist the devil, he will _____?
   Fight, Fuss, Mislead, Flee
3. "A word fitly spoken is like apples of gold in pictures of . . ."?
   Song, Silver, Meadows, Eden
4. Who was quoted, "Is there any taste in the white of an egg"?
   Solomon, David, Daniel, Job
5. What did Job behold as the fear of the Lord?
   Distrust, Wisdom, Unrighteousness, Sympathy
6. Eber was a great-grandson of Noah's son Shem and the father of . . .?
   Parosh, Padon, Peleg, Peter

ANSWERS:

1. Old (Thirty-third book in the Old Testament)
2. Flee (James 4:7)
3. Silver (Proverbs 25:11)
4. Job (Job 6:6)
5. Wisdom (Job 28:28)
6. Peleg (Genesis 10:25)

Score Correct: _____ Date: _____ Name: _____

Study Notes: _____

_____

_____

Quiz 66

1. Is the book of Ashkelon in the Old Testament, New Testament, or neither?
2. Who killed sixty-nine of his brethren, but spared Jotham "for he hid himself"?
   Abimelech, Jeroboam, Uzziah, Horam
3. Which angel fights against Satan in the book of Revelation?
   Gabriel, Cherubim, Elohim, Michael
4. Who was Ananias's wife who died along with her husband after lying about an offering?
   Jezebel, Anna, Sapphira, Jael
5. Who said, "God hath shewed me that I should not call any man common or unclean"?
   Adam, Reuben, Samson, Peter
6. Who was first of the twelve disciples to be murdered?
   Peter, Thomas, Judas, James

ANSWERS:

1. Neither (Coastal city in Southern District of Israel)
2. Abimelech (Judges 9:4–5)
3. Michael (Revelation 12:7–9)
4. Sapphira (Acts 5:1–11)
5. Peter (Acts 10:26–28)
6. James (Acts 12:1–2)

Score Correct: _____ Date: _____ Name: _____
Study Notes: _____
_____
_____

Quiz 67

1. Is the book of Bethany in the Old Testament, New Testament, or neither?
2. Which mount was a contest scene between Elijah and the prophets of Baal?
    Calvary, Sinai, Bethel, Carmel
3. What Moabite woman became ancestress of King David through her marriage to Boaz?
    Sarah, Jezebel, Ruth, Leah
4. Which city is often referred to as Zion?
    Bethlehem, Jericho, Jerusalem, Nazareth
5. Who said, "My soul doth magnify the Lord"?
    Ruth, Sarah, Miriam, Mary
6. What tribe of Israel was Saul, son of Kish, from?
    Ephraim, Gad, Issachar, Benjamin

ANSWERS:
1. Neither (Palestinian town bordering East Jerusalem)
2. Carmel (1 Kings 18:19–38)
3. Ruth (Ruth 4:9–10)
4. Jerusalem (Isaiah 30:19)
5. Mary (Luke 1:46)
6. Benjamin (1 Samuel 9:21)

Score Correct: _____ Date: _____ Name: _____
Study Notes: _____
_____
_____

Quiz 68

1. Is the book of Nehemiah in the Old Testament, New Testament, or neither?
2. Which New Testament woman holds the record for widowhood at eighty-four years?
   Abigail, Anna, Lydia, Priscilla
3. What was the site for Moses's burial place?
   Paphos, Bethpeor, Petra, Beth-shan
4. From 2 Samuel, who said "Thou art the man"?
   Boaz, Samson, Isaac, Nathan
5. Who was the father of the Apostles James and John?
   Zechariah, Zephaniah, Zebedee, Zebulun
6. How many mites (copper coins) make a farthing?
   2, 4, 6, 8

ANSWERS:
1. Old (Sixteenth book of the Old Testament)
2. Anna (Luke 2:36–37)
3. Bethpeor (Deuteronomy 34:6)
4. Nathan (2 Samuel 12:7)
5. Zebedee (Matthew 4:21)
6. 2 (Mark 12:4)

Score Correct: _____ Date: _____ Name: _____
Study Notes: _____
_____
_____

Quiz 69

1. Is the book of 1 Thessalonians in the Old Testament, New Testament, or neither?
2. Who said, "Be sure your sin will find you out"?
    Matthew, David, Noah, Moses
3. From the book of 1 Kings, who built the walls of Jerusalem?
    Ezekiel, Rahab, Jael, Solomon
4. From scripture, "Can the Ethiopian change his skin, or the _____ his spots"?
    Tiger, Zebra, Cheetah, Leopard
5. Who supplied the five loaves and two fish that Jesus used to feed a multitude of five thousand?
    Andrew, A lad, Simon Peter, Philip
6. Who was the warrior, Barak, the son of?
    Abdeel, Abel, Abinoam, Amos

ANSWERS:
1. New (Thirteenth book of the New Testament)
2. Moses (Numbers 32:20–23)
3. Solomon (1 Kings 9:15)
4. Leopard (Jeremiah 13:23)
5. A lad (John 6:9 - 11
6. Abinoam (Judges 4:6)

Score Correct: _____ Date: _____ Name: _____
Study Notes: _____
_____
_____

Quiz 70

1. Is the book of Titus in the Old Testament, New Testament, or neither?
2. The Year of Jubilee comes around once every how many years?
   5, 25, 50, 75
3. Who's the first person whose death is mentioned in the book of Exodus?
   Joseph, Aaron, Moses, Yahweh
4. How long had the woman been sick that touched the hem of Jesus's garment?
   6 years, 6 months, 12 years, 12 months
5. In scripture who was the first individual killed by God for being wicked?
   No One, Er, Onan, Gomorrah
6. Which prophet experienced an earthquake while standing on a mountaintop?
   Elijah, Abraham, James, Thomas

ANSWERS:

1. New (Seventeenth book of the New Testament)
2. 50 (Leviticus 25:11)
3. Joseph (Exodus 1:6)
4. 12 years (Mark 5: 25–29)
5. Er (Genesis 38:7)
6. Elijah (1 Kings 19:1–11)

Score Correct: _____ Date: _____ Name: _____
Study Notes: _____
_____
_____

Quiz 71

1. Is the book of Joshua in the Old Testament, New Testament, or neither?
2. Who had a vision of heaven opening with a certain vessel descending, as it had been a great sheet knit of four corners?
   Caleb, Peter, Paul, Samson
3. "The Lord is my strength and my shield" is in which Psalm?
   8, 18, 28, 38
4. Who was the husband of Priscilla?
   Atilla, Aquila, Andrew, Alpheus
5. Who recounts the story of Abraham along with the captivity and freedom of the children of Israel?
   Paul, Peter, Stephen, Andrew
6. Who or what type of person was Bar-jesus?
   Cousin of Jesus, Early Priest, Sorcerer, Associate of Paul

ANSWERS:

1. Old (Sixth book of the Old Testament)
2. Peter (Acts 10:9–11)
3. 28 (Psalms 28:7)
4. Aquila (Acts 18:2)
5. Stephen (Acts 6:8, 7:1–36)
6. Sorcerer (Acts 13:6)

Score Correct: _____ Date: _____ Name: _____
Study Notes: _____
_____
_____

Quiz 72

1. Is the book of Zareathites in the Old Testament, New Testament, or neither?
2. What bird, found in Egypt today and commonly called "Pharaoh's chicken," is mentioned only twice?
   Gier Eagle, Lapwing, Ospray, Cormorant
3. Who asked of the Lord, "Am I my brother's keeper"?
   Abel, Cain, Joseph, Seth
4. Who was exiled to the land of Nod?
   Cain, Abel, Abraham, Aaron
5. Which businesswoman from Thyatira opened her home to Paul after her conversion?
   Lydia, Rachel, Keturah, Shiphrah
6. The superscription "This Is the King of The Jews" was written over Jesus on the cross in how many different languages?
   2, 3, 4, 5

ANSWERS:

1. Neither (Inhabitants of Zareah or Zorah)
2. Gier Eagle (Leviticus 11:18 and Deuteronomy 14:17)
3. Cain (Genesis 4:9)
4. Cain (Genesis 4:16)
5. Lydia (Acts 16:14, 37–40)
6. 3 (Luke 23:38)

Score Correct: _____ Date: _____ Name: _____
Study Notes: _____
_____
_____

Quiz 73

1. Is the book of Isaiah in the Old Testament, New Testament, or neither?
2. Who was the first king of Israel?
   David, Saul, Solomon, Jehu
3. Who denied Jesus three times in the book of John?
   John, James, Luke, Peter
4. From Genesis 21, who put her child under a shrub to die?
   Hagar, Miriam, Ezra, Sarah
5. Jesus said, "For where your treasure is, there will be your _____ also."
   Love, Heart, Faith, Friends
6. What did the crowds repeat on Jesus's triumphal entry into Jerusalem?
   Hallelujah, Hosanna, Amen, Messiah

ANSWERS:
1. Old (Twenty-third book of the Old Testament)
2. Saul (1 Samuel 9:16–17)
3. Peter (John 13:37–38)
4. Hagar (Genesis 21:14–15)
5. Heart (Luke 12:34)
6. Hosanna (John 12:12–13)

Score Correct: _____ Date: _____ Name: _____
Study Notes: _____
_____
_____

Quiz 74

1. Is the book of Elisabeth in the Old Testament, New Testament, or neither?
2. At what age did Uzziah become king of Jerusalem?
   16, 36, 66, 96
3. Which prophet saw a man (the Lord's angel) riding on a red horse?
   Zechariah, Hosea, Nathan, Isaiah
4. Which son of David was known for his good looks?
   Ibhar, Amnon, Nogah, Absalom
5. What was Adam's occupation in Eden?
   Preacher, Shepherd, Carpenter, Gardener
6. Who had a vision of a barley cake tumbling into an army camp and overturning a tent?
   Shepherd, Man (Soldier), Peasant, Steward (Boy)

ANSWERS:

1. Neither (Wife of Zacharias and mother of John the Baptist)
2. 16 (2 Chronicles 26:3)
3. Zechariah (Zechariah 1:8–10)
4. Absalom (2 Samuel 13:1, 14:25)
5. Gardener (Genesis 2:15)
6. Man (Soldier) (Judges 7:13)

Score Correct: _____ Date: _____ Name: _____
Study Notes: _____
_____
_____

Quiz 75

1. Is the book of Hosea in the Old Testament, New Testament, or neither?
2. Which Old Testament book foretold the giving of vinegar to Jesus on the cross?
   Exodus, Ruth, Job, Psalms
3. Where did the apostles go after an angel had delivered them from a Jerusalem prison?
   Temple, Fields, Mountaintop, River
4. In a vision, who was suspended between heaven and earth by a lock of hair?
   Samson, Esau, Elijah, Ezekiel
5. What is the longest book of the Old Testament by most number of chapters?
   Esther, Job, Psalms, Proverbs
6. How did God identify himself when He spoke to Moses from the burning bush?
   Lord God of Israel, Jesus Christ, I Am That I Am, Jehovah

ANSWERS:

1. Old (Twenty-eighth book of the Old Testament)
2. Psalms (Psalms 69:21)
3. Temple (Acts 5:19–20)
4. Ezekiel (Ezekiel 8:3)
5. Psalms (150 chapters)
6. I Am That I Am (Exodus 3:4, 14)

Score Correct: _____ Date: _____ Name: _____
Study Notes: _____
_____
_____

Quiz 76

1. Is the book of Haggai in the Old Testament, New Testament, or neither?
2. Who had a vision of angels climbing up and down a ladder reaching into heaven?
   Joseph, Ahab, Ehud, Jacob
3. What does Paul say is the supreme gift of the prophecies to believers?
   Charity, Hope, Faith, Eternity
4. Where did Jesus turn water into wine?
   Bethany, Nazareth, Cana, Gethsemane
5. What's the shield to "quench all the fiery darts of the wicked"?
   Belief, Love, Compassion, Faith
6. Who lost his massive strength after given a haircut?
   Samson, Pharaoh, Noah, Matthew

ANSWERS:

1. Old (Thirty-seventh book of the Old Testament)
2. Jacob (Genesis 28:10–12)
3. Charity (1 Corinthians 1:1; 13:8, 13)
4. Cana (John 2:10–11)
5. Faith (Ephesians 6:16)
6. Samson (Judges 16:19–20)

Score Correct: _____ Date: _____ Name: _____
Study Notes: _____
_____
_____

Quiz 77

1. Is the book of Ozni in the Old Testament, New Testament, or neither?
2. Where do we learn, "There is neither Jew nor Greek ... slave nor free ... male nor female ... for we are all one in Christ Jesus"?
   Luke, Galatians, Titus, 1 Peter
3. Which son of Cain had a city named after him?
   Japheth, Enoch, Haran, Jethro
4. Who was Paul's companion at Philippi?
   Stephen, Jude, Silas, Luke
5. What woman defied her husband to provide food for David's men in the wilderness?
   Esther, Abigail, Lydia, Ruth
6. Who was the first apostle chosen by Jesus?
   Simon (Peter), Andrew, Thomas, John

ANSWERS:
1. Neither (One of the descendants of Gad)
2. Galatians (Galatians 3:28)
3. Enoch (Genesis 4:17)
4. Silas (Acts 16:19–23)
5. Abigail (1 Samuel 25:18–24)
6. Simon (Peter) (Matthew 10:1–2)

Score Correct: _____ Date: _____ Name: _____
Study Notes: _____
_____
_____

Quiz 78

1. Is the book of Rama in the Old Testament, New Testament, or neither?
2. Who, while Sisera was sleeping, went softly to him and smote a nail into his temples, killing him?
   Jael, Huldah, Rahab, Dinah
3. By what work did Paul support his ministry?
   Shepherd, Carpenter, Tentmaker, Stonemason
4. What Roman officer was instructed in a vision to contact Simon Peter?
   Marcus, Maximus, Quintus, Cornelius
5. Who escaped on horseback from enemy Israelites?
   Benhadad, Lazarus, Haman, Dathan
6. What was Judas Iscariot's duty among the apostles?
   Cook, Treasurer, Foot Cleaner, Carpenter

ANSWERS:
1. Neither (City near Gibeah of Benjamin)
2. Jael (Judges 4:17–18, 21–22)
3. Tentmaker (Acts 18:1–3)
4. Cornelius (Acts 10:3–5)
5. Benhadad (I Kings 20:20)
6. Treasurer (John 12:4–6)

Score Correct: _____ Date: _____ Name: _____
Study Notes: _____
_____
_____

Quiz 79

1. Is the book of Nebo in the Old Testament, New Testament, or neither?
2. Which of Satan's temptations of Jesus involved a "pinnacle of the temple"?
   None, First, Second, Third
3. What tentmaking couple offered hospitality to Paul in Corinth?
   Priscilla/Aquila, Naomi/Elimelech, Mary/Joseph, Ruth/Boaz
4. Which Pharisee was a doctor of law?
   Paul, Jonathan, Hillel, Gamaliel
5. David was his father, but who was King Solomon's mother?
   Sheba, Bathsheba, Kish, Esther
6. What number descendant of Adam was Noah?
   Second, Third, Sixth, Ninth

ANSWERS:

1. Neither (A mountain in the land of Moab)
2. Second (Matthew 4:3–7)
3. Priscilla/Aquila (Acts 18: 14–26
4. Gamaliel (Acts 5:34)
5. Bathsheba (2 Samuel 12:24)
6. Ninth (Genesis 5:1–29)

Score Correct: _____ Date: _____ Name: _____
Study Notes: _____
_____
_____

Quiz 80

1. Is the book of Esther in the Old Testament, New Testament, or neither?
2. From the book of Revelation, the seven churches are in what Roman province?
   Sardis, Philadelphia, Patmos, Asia
3. Who was confronted by priests and Levites when confessing, "I am not the Christ"?
   Paul, Andrew, John, Joshua
4. From the book of Genesis, how many stars made obeisance to Joseph in a dream?
   0, 1, 11, 20
5. Who had his servants dig a well after building an altar at Beersheba?
   Isaac, Elijah, Josiah, Gideon
6. Who fell dead after lying about a property deal?
   Lazarus, Ananias, Ehud, Koran

ANSWERS:
1. Old (Seventeenth book of the Old Testament, and one of two books named after a woman)
2. Asia (Revelation 1:4)
3. John (John 1:15–20)
4. 11 (Genesis 37:5, 9)
5. Isaac (Genesis 26:25)
6. Ananias (Acts 5:1–6)

Score Correct: _____ Date: _____ Name: _____
Study Notes: _____
_____
_____

Joseph's dreams
Courtesy of: clipart.christiansunite.com

Quiz 81

1. Is the book of Ichabod in the Old Testament, New Testament, or neither?
2. To evade a famine, Abram and his wife Sarai entered into Egypt, and Abram, to save his life, pretended that Sarai was his . . . ?
   Mother, Neighbor, Sister, Daughter
3. What was the total number of wives, princesses, and three hundred concubines of King Solomon?
   50, 100, 200, 700
4. In Psalms, what type of cymbals are described to praise Him?
   High sounding, Gold, Ones from Babylon, Silver
5. What did Cain, the first son of Adam and Eve, do for a living?
   Carpenter, Keeper of sheep, Tiller of the ground, Tentmaker
6. Who was the first son of Moses and Zipporah?
   Haggai, Gershom, Mark, Zebudah

ANSWERS:

1. Neither (Son of Phinehas killed in battle of Aphek)
2. Sister (Genesis 12:10–13)
3. 700 (1 Kings 11:1–3)
4. High sounding (Psalms 150:5)
5. Tiller of the ground (Genesis 4:1–2)
6. Gershom (Exodus 2:21–22)

Score Correct: _____ Date: _____ Name: _____
Study Notes: _____
_____
_____

Quiz 82

1. Is the book of Ahiam in the Old Testament, New Testament, or neither?
2. Which wielding piece of the armor of God to stand against the wiles of the devil is "the word of God"?
   Breastplate of righteousness, Sword of the Spirit, Shield of faith, Gospel of peace
3. Who witnessed Elijah's ascent into heaven by a whirlwind?
   Kings Ahab, Elisha, King Ahaziah, Jehu
4. Which two gospels feature the Lord's Prayer?
   Matthew, Mark, Luke, John
5. James reminds us to be slow to speak and slow to . . . ?
   Hear, Scorn, Gossip, Wrath
6. Which book follows Nahum?
   Obadiah, Habakkuk, Haggai, Joel

ANSWERS:

1. Neither (Sharar's son and a warrior among David's men)
2. Sword of the Spirit (Ephesians 6:11, 17)
3. Elisha (2 Kings 2: 11–12)
4. Matthew/Luke (Matthew 6:9–13, Luke 11:1–4)
5. Wrath (James 1:19)
6. Habakkuk (Thirty-fifth book of the Old Testament)

Score Correct: _____ Date: _____ Name: _____
Study Notes: _____

_____

_____

Quiz 83

1. Is the book of Centurion in the Old Testament, New Testament, or neither?
2. Who hid a hundred prophets in two caves and supplied them with food and water?
   Solomon, Philemon, Obadiah, Hosea
3. Solomon said what "biteth like a serpent, and stingeth like an adder"?
   Woman's scorn, Evil brother, Tax collector, Wine
4. On the island of Patmos, to whom was the book of Revelation given?
   John, Paul, Matthew, Luke
5. In Psalms, what are the dove's feathers covered with?
   White manna, Yellow gold, Brown leaves, Red blood
6. What name did Jesus give to Simon Peter?
   Macedonia, Nahu, Cephas, Eli

ANSWERS:

1. Neither (A Roman military officer who commanded one hundred men)
2. Obadiah (1 Kings 18:4)
3. Wine (Proverbs 23:31–32)
4. John the Revelator (Revelation 1:1, 9)
5. Yellow gold (Psalms 68:13)
6. Cephas (John 1:42)

Score Correct: _____ Date: _____ Name: _____
Study Notes: _____
_____
_____

Quiz 84

1. Is the book of Ur in the Old Testament, New Testament, or neither?
2. Emboldened by God's declaration, which Old Testament king went into battle with singers leading the army?
   Ahaz, Hezekiah, Manasseh, Jehoshaphat
3. What name did Nebuchadnezzar give to Daniel?
   Eliasaph, Jakim, Belteshazzar, Omar
4. "God wrought special miracles by the hands of _____"?
   Manahen, Zechariah, Paul, Silas
5. On the outskirts of what city did Jesus meet Zacchaeus?
   Smyrna, Tarsus, Jericho, Antioch
6. Who was the mother of the prophet Samuel?
   Peninnah, Hannah, Sarah, Deborah

ANSWERS:

1. Neither (A great sacred cemetery city near the mouth of the Euphrates)
2. Jehoshaphat (2 Chronicles 20:18–21)
3. Belteshazzar (Daniel 1:1, 7)
4. Paul (Acts 19:11)
5. Jericho (Luke 19:1–5)
6. Hannah (1 Samuel 1:20)

Score Correct: _____ Date: _____ Name: _____
Study Notes: _____
_____
_____

Quiz 85

1. Is the book of Jeremiah in the Old Testament, New Testament, or neither?
2. From the Law of Moses, how long was a woman considered unclean after she gave birth to a female?
   3 days, 7 days, 2 weeks, 4 weeks
3. Where were the bodies of Saul and his sons nailed to a wall?
   Nob, Bethshan, Nob, Sychar
4. In Proverbs, he that loveth wine and oil shall not be_____?
   Blamed, Loved, Pure, Rich
5. Nadab and Abihu were the sons of whom?
   Moses, Noah, Aaron, Isaac
6. On what day did God create the evening and the morning?
   3rd, 4th, 5th, 6th

ANSWERS:
1. Old (Twenty-fourth book of the Old Testament)
2. 2 weeks (Leviticus 12:1, 5)
3. Bethshan (1 Samuel 31:2, 10, 12)
4. Rich (Proverbs 21:17)
5. Aaron (Leviticus 10:1)
6. 4th (Genesis 1:19)

Score Correct: _____ Date: _____ Name: _____
Study Notes: _____
_____
_____

Quiz 86

1. Is the book of Baalis in the Old Testament, New Testament, or neither?
2. Which book repeats this paraphrased counsel three times to the young women of Jerusalem, "Do not stir up or awaken love until it pleases"?
   Proverbs, Psalms, Song of Solomon, Genesis
3. Who said, "I have heard many such things: miserable comforters are ye all"?
   Beelzebub, Job, Jesus, John the Baptist
4. At which church was Paul accused of turning the world upside down?
   Smyrna, Antioch, Sardis, Thessalonica
5. From Psalms, "The Lord is my light and my _____"?
   Rock, Glory, Salvation, Anointed
6. Who built Elath and restored it to Judah?
   David, Nimrod, Azariah, Hiel

ANSWERS:

1. Neither (Ammonite king)
2. Song of Solomon (Song of Solomon 2:7, 3:5, 8:4)
3. Job (Job 16:2)
4. Thessalonica (Acts 17:1, 6)
5. Salvation (Psalms 27:1)
6. Azariah (2 Kings 14:21–22)

Score Correct: _____ Date: _____ Name: _____

Study Notes: _____

_____

_____

Quiz 87

1. Is the book of Paseah in the Old Testament, New Testament, or neither?
2. Who did the island people of Melita (Malta) think was a god when he was unaffected by the viper's bite?
   Job, Paul, Timothy, Stephen
3. Which tribe of Israel was to be like an adder (snake) that biteth the horse heels?
   Asher, Issachar, Zebulun, Dan
4. Of whom did Naaman the Syrian ask forgiveness after worshipping the god Rimmon?
   Saul, Christ, Elisha, Darius
5. In which book is the phrase "holier than thou"?
   2 Kings, Ezra, Amos, Isaiah
6. Whose four daughters were considered prophetesses?
   Gad, Philip, Jonah, Noah

ANSWERS:

1. Neither (Son of Eshton and descendant of Judah)
2. Paul (Acts 28:1–6)
3. Dan (Genesis 49:16–17)
4. Elisha (2 Kings 5:18–20)
5. Isaiah (Isaiah 65:5)
6. Philip (Acts 21:8–9)

Score Correct: _____ Date: _____ Name: _____
Study Notes: _____
_____
_____

Quiz 88

1. Is the book of Darius in the Old Testament, New Testament, or neither?
2. How many arrows did Joash smite (shoot) into the ground at Elisha's command?
   1, 2, 3, 4
3. What did Jesus warn against casting (throwing) to pigs?
   Bread, Bones, Pearls, Rocks
4. Which city is associated with Joshua and the blowing of the trumpets?
   Capernaum, Jericho, Seleucia, Nicopolis
5. What does the shortest verse in the Bible say Jesus did?
   Cried, Prayed, Wept, Roamed
6. Who was the father of Elkanah?
   Jeremiah, Philip, Esau, Jeroham

ANSWERS:

1. Neither (Name of three emperors of the Persian dynasty)
2. 3 (2 Kings 13:14–18)
3. Pearls (Matthew 7:6)
4. Jericho (Joshau 6:1–5)
5. Wept (John 11:35)
6. Jeroham (1 Samuel 1:1)

Score Correct: _____ Date: _____ Name: _____
Study Notes: _____
_____
_____

Quiz 89

1. Is the book of Diviners in the Old Testament, New Testament, or neither?
2. Which body part does Paul call "beautiful" on those that preach the gospel of peace and bring glad tidings?
   Tongue, Heart, Hands, Feet
3. Who was the left-handed Benjamite that killed Eglon?
   Geshem, Agag, Ehud, Joram
4. What did Isaiah say shall be upon the shoulder of Jesus?
   Firewood, The government, Lightning, Children
5. Who purified a pot of deadly stew with meal (flour)?
   Josiah, Elisha, Jehu, Hilkiah
6. Whose biblical name means "messenger"?
   Aaron, Moses, Samuel, Malachi

ANSWERS:

1. Neither (Like soothsayers, persons believed to tell the future)
2. Feet (Romans 10:15)
3. Ehud (Judges 3:15–21)
4. The government (Isaiah 9:6)
5. Elisha (2 Kings 4:38–41)
6. Malachi (Malachi 1:1, 3:1)

Score Correct: _____ Date: _____ Name: _____
Study Notes: _____
_____
_____

Quiz 90

1. Is the book of Ararat in the Old Testament, New Testament, or neither?
2. From Proverbs, what same word goes into both blanks, "_____ sharpeneth _____, and one man sharpeneth the countenance of his friend"?
   Razor, Gold, Tongue, Iron
3. Who stretched himself upon the widow's son to bring him back to life?
   Lazarus, Elijah, Bartholomew, Cyrus
4. Machpelah, Makkedah, and Adullam are specific names of . . . ?
   Demons, Waterfalls, Valleys, Caves
5. What caused Jonah's sheltering plant (gourd) to wither?
   Worm, Locust, Sun, Wind
6. The seven sons of Sceva were fake . . . ?
   Shepherds, Exorcists, Tentmakers, Soldiers

ANSWERS:

1. Neither (Country on one of the mountains where the Ark rested after the Flood subsided)
2. Iron (Proverbs 27:17)
3. Elijah (1 Kings 17:18–22)
4. Caves (Genesis 23:9, Joshua 10:16, 1 Samuel 22:1)
5. Worm (Jonah 4:6–7)
6. Exorcists (Acts 19:13–15)

Score Correct: _____ Date: _____ Name: _____
Study Notes: _____
_____
_____

Quiz 91

1. Is the book of Rahab in the Old Testament, New Testament, or neither?
2. Jesus said, "For even the Son of man came not to be ministered unto, but to minister, and to give his life a _____ for many."
   Reason, Ransom, Reward, Return
3. How did the paralyzed man's friends present him through the crowds to get to Jesus?
   Donkey-pulled cart, Lowered through roof, Pulled up stairs, Trumpets blaring
4. What was the first thing Noah did after leaving the ark?
   Burned it, Built an altar, Performed a marriage, Hiked to mountains
5. What group did John the Baptist exhort to be content with their wages?
   Priests, Zealots, Judges, Soldiers
6. Which king of Israel had a reputation as a wild chariot driver?
   Jehoahaz, Jehoash, Jehu, Jehoram

ANSWERS:

1. Neither (Wife of Salmon and mother of Boaz)
2. Ransom (Mark 10:45)
3. Lowered through roof (Mark 2:3–5)
4. Built an altar (Genesis 8:20)
5. Soldiers (Luke 3:14–15)
6. Jehu (2 Kings 9:20)

Score Correct: _____ Date: _____ Name: _____
Study Notes: _____

_____

_____

Quiz 92

1. Is the book of Naamah in the Old Testament, New Testament, or neither?
2. From 2 Samuel, who asked, "How are the mighty fallen, and the weapons of war perished"?
   Saul, Simeon, David, Peter
3. Which prophet foretold the ministry of John the Baptist?
   Shemaiah, Isaiah, Mordecai, Levi
4. When being stoned, who said, "Lord, lay not this sin to their charge"?
   Philip, Stephen, Luke, David
5. From the Beatitudes, who shall be called the children of God?
   Hungry, Peacemakers, Merciful, Lonely
6. Which book follows 3 John?
   1 Peter, Philemon, Jude, 1 Timothy

ANSWERS:

1. Neither (Daughter of Lamech and Zillah)
2. David (2 Samuel 1:16, 27)
3. Isaiah (Isaiah 40:3, Matthew 3:1, Mark 1:3)
4. Stephen (Acts 7:59–60)
5. Peacemakers (Matthew 5:9)
6. Jude (Twenty-sixth book of the New Testament)

Score Correct: _____ Date: _____ Name: _____

Study Notes: _____

_____

_____

Quiz 93

1. Is the book of Omer in the Old Testament, New Testament, or neither?
2. From 2 Samuel, who received a letter from David telling him to put Uriah into battle?
   Gideon, Ahab, Isaac, Joab
3. Why was Daniel thrown into the lions' den by King Darius?
   War spy, Caught praying to God, Deep in debt, Affair with king's daughter
4. Luke said Jesus was about how old when he began to teach?
   16, 19, 24, 30
5. Which disciple stole from the treasury?
   Thomas, Judas, James, John
6. How old was Abraham when he died?
   81, 175, 206, 300

ANSWERS:

1. Neither (Ancient Hebrew dry measurement, the tenth part of an ephah)
2. Joab (2 Samuel 11:14–15)
3. Caught praying to God (Daniel 6:7–11)
4. 30 (Luke 3:23)
5. Judas (John 12:4–6)
6. 175 (Genesis 25:7)

Score Correct: _____ Date: _____ Name: _____
Study Notes: _____
_____
_____

Quiz 94

1. Is the book of Pisgah in the Old Testament, New Testament, or neither?
2. What was Jesus weeping over in the Bible's shortest verse, "Jesus wept"?
   His impending death, Sins of the people, Death of Lazarus, Fall of Jericho
3. Which two disciples asked Jesus if they could sit on his right and his left?
   Philip, James, Thomas, John
4. Samson was put into prison as a political enemy of whom?
   Romans, Israelites, Philistines, Assyrians
5. From Matthew 17, who did Jesus send fishing to find tax money?
   Andrew, Peter, Paul, Judas
6. Who did Ruth marry after the death of her first husband Mahlon?
   Isaiah, Ahab, Boaz, Jehu

ANSWERS:
1. Neither (Mountain summit in the land of Moab)
2. Death of Lazarus (John 11:14, 31–35)
3. James and John (Mark 10:35–37)
4. Philistines (Judges 16:20–21)
5. Peter (Matthew 17:24–27)
6. Boaz (Ruth 4:10, 13)

Score Correct: _____ Date: _____ Name: _____
Study Notes: _____
_____
_____

Quiz 95

1. Is the book of Pekah in the Old Testament, New Testament, or neither?
2. Where is the phrase, "For whatsoever a man soweth, that shall he also reap," found?
   Ephesians, Colossians, Galatians, 1 Timothy
3. What prophet approached Joseph and Mary when they took the child Jesus to the temple?
   Miriam, Anna, Noadiah, Huldah
4. Who asked God, "Why is my pain perpetual, and my wound incurable"?
   Moses, Jeremiah, Abraham, Noah
5. How many angels rescued Lot and his family from Sodom?
   2, 7, 13, Heavenly host
6. Where is the story of the burning bush found?
   Genesis, Exodus, Luke, John

ANSWERS:

1. Neither (Son of Remaliah and a king of Israel)
2. Galatians (Galatians 6:7)
3. Anna (Luke 2:27, 36)
4. Jeremiah (Jeremiah 15:18)
5. 2 (Genesis 19:1)
6. Exodus (Exodus 3:1–6)

Score Correct: _____ Date: _____ Name: _____
Study Notes: _____
_____
_____

Quiz 96

1. Is the book of Daniel in the Old Testament, New Testament, or neither?
2. Which woman became frustrated when she was left to serve Jesus by herself after she received Him into her house?
   Esther, Martha, Naomi, Tabitha
3. Why did Pharaoh's daughter name her adopted son Moses?
   Crying profusely, Light-colored hair, Drew him out of water, Basket sinking
4. From Psalms, "God is our refuge and _____, a very present help in trouble."
   Saviour, Light, Strength, Salvation
5. Aaron's sons were chosen to be priests because his staff . . . ?
   Glowed, Turned into a viper, Rained and thundered, Grew flowers
6. What did Jesus say are better arrayed than Solomon in all his glory?
   Lilies, Angels, Trees, Sheep

ANSWERS:

1. Old (Twenty-seventh book of the Old Testament)
2. Martha (Luke 10:38–40)
3. Drew him out of water (Exodus 2:9–10)
4. Strength (Psalms 46:1)
5. Grew flowers (Numbers 17:2–8)
6. Lilies (Luke 12:27)

Score Correct: _____ Date: _____ Name: _____
Study Notes: _____
_____
_____

Quiz 97

1. Is the book of Asiel in the Old Testament, New Testament, or neither?
2. What happened to Jeroboam's hand on confronting the man of God at the altar?
   Fell off, Turned to salt, Became a viper, Dried up
3. The forty-two children making fun of Elisha's bald head were torn apart by?
   Two she bears, Three lions, Seven serpents, Locust swarm
4. What size faith did Jesus say was needed, as a grain of what type of seed?
   Wheat, Mustard, Pear, Apple
5. From Acts, who was called "A man after mine own heart"?
   Gideon, David, Matthew, James
6. On what day did God create the birds (fowl)?
   1st, 2nd, 3rd, 5th

ANSWERS:

1. Neither (Jehu's great-grandfather)
2. Dried up (1 Kings 13:1–4)
3. Two she bears (2 Kings 2:19, 23–24)
4. Mustard (Matthew 17:20)
5. David (Acts 13:22)
6. 5th (Genesis 1:20, 23)

Score Correct: _____ Date: _____ Name: _____
Study Notes: _____
_____
_____

Quiz 98

1. Is the book of Eutychus in the Old Testament, New Testament, or neither?
2. Who told Queen Esther that she has a unique opportunity to act on behalf of the Jewish people?
    Mordecai, Amyrtaeus, Vashti, Ahasuerus
3. Whose daughter demanded John the Baptist's head on a platter?
    Herodias, Laban, Herod, Naaman
4. What did Samuel's mother bring him when she visited year after year?
    Sweet cake, Letters from friends, Flute, Little coat
5. Who was the greedy servant of Elisha who became cursed and leprous?
    Gehazi, Mephibosheth, Onesimus, Bilhah
6. From Joshua 12, how many kings did Joshua defeat in battle?
    8, 19, 20 and 2, 30 and 1

ANSWERS:

1. Neither (Young boy who falls from a window and dies, but through a miracle is resurrected)
2. Mordecai (Esther 4:13–14)
3. Herodias (Matthew 14:6–8)
4. Little coat (robe) (1 Samuel 2:18–19)
5. Gehazi (2 Kings 5:25–27)
6. 30 and 1 (Joshua 12:7, 9–24)

Score Correct: _____ Date: _____ Name: _____
Study Notes: _____
_____
_____

Quiz 99

1. Is the book of Gihon in the Old Testament, New Testament, or neither?
2. Which king decreed that people should only pray to him for the next thirty days, and if not, they were to be cast into the den of lions?
   Darius, Elah, Omri, Ahaziah
3. Who had a vision of a sea of glass like unto crystal?
   Thomas, John, Peter, Nicodemus
4. Who was the baby born of Zacharias and Elizabeth?
   Daniel, John (the Baptist), Noah, David
5. In Exodus, what creatures came up from the waters in abundance?
   Serpents, Frogs, Fishes, Eels
6. There were how many generations from Abraham to Jesus?
   12, 26, 42, 54

ANSWERS:

1. Neither (One of the four rivers of Eden)
2. Darius (Daniel 6:7–9)
3. John (Revelation 4:6)
4. John (the Baptist) (Luke 1:13)
5. Frogs (Exodus 8:3–6)
6. 42 (Matthew 1:1 -16)

Score Correct: _____ Date: _____ Name: _____
Study Notes: _____
_____
_____

Quiz 100

1. Is the book of Bernice in the Old Testament, New Testament, or neither?
2. On which side of the ship did Jesus tell the disciples to cast their net to find the multitude of fishes?
   Sunny, Windward, Left, Right
3. Who was the centurion of Augustus's band that escorted Paul to Italy by boat?
   Julius, Cornelius, Phineas, Jephthah
4. As he stole treasures from Jericho, who was called "the troubler of Israel"?
   Gestas, Achan, Dismas, Rakh
5. What do the seven candlesticks represent in the book of Revelation?
   Demons, Churches, Rivers, Valleys
6. Besore, Arnon, and Gaash are specifically referred to as . . . ?
   Mountains, Camels, Inns, Brooks

ANSWERS:

1. Neither (Daughter of King Agrippa I)
2. Right (John 21:1, 5–6)
3. Julius (Acts 27:1)
4. Achan (Also called Achar) (Joshua 7:21, 24–25, 1 Chronicles 2:7)
5. Churches (Revelation 1:20)
6. Brooks (1 Samuel 30:9, Numbers 21:14, 1 Chronicles 11:32)

Score Correct: _____ Date: _____ Name: _____
Study Notes: _____
_____
_____

Apostles preaching the Gospel
Courtesy of: clipart.christiansunite.com

Quiz 101

1. Is the book of Kabzeel in the Old Testament, New Testament, or neither?
2. How many stones did the Lord tell the nation of Israel to gather to make a memorial after they passed over the Jordan? 7, 12, 24, 49
3. What were the rattling and shaking sounds Ezekiel heard when he prophesized in the valley?
   Wind through branches, Skeleton army marching, Dry bones coming together, Multitude of rattlesnakes moving
4. In Song of Solomon, a woman's hair is compared to a flock of? Doves, Crows, Ravens, Goats
5. What caused Paul's boat to shipwreck at Melita (Malta)? Pirates, Mighty wave, Old sunken ship, Reef
6. In Ezekiel, what kind of heart does God say he will give His people?
   Compassionate, Of flesh, Sincere, Of love

ANSWERS:

1. Neither (Remote city of Judah; located on the border of Edom)
2. 12 (Joshua 4:1–7, 20–24)
3. Dry bones coming together (Ezekiel 37:1–9)
4. Goats (Song of Solomon 4:1)
5. Reef (Acts 27:9, 40–41, Acts 28:1)
6. Of flesh (Ezekiel 11:19, 36:23–26)

Score Correct: _____ Date: _____ Name: _____
Study Notes: _____
_____
_____

Quiz 102

1. Is the book of 1 Samuel in the Old Testament, New Testament, or neither?
2. Who used the excuse, "My family is poor in Manasseh, and I am the least in my father's house"?
   Aaron, David, Gideon, Jeroboam
3. With what kind of leaves did Adam and Eve attempt to cover their nakedness?
   Sycamore, Fig, Palm, Grape
4. From Judges 7, with how many men did Gideon defeat the Midianites?
   3, 30, 300, 3000
5. Who was the father of Joshua?
   Samuel, Nun, Jesse, Aaron
6. What was the homeland of Job?
   Thyatira, Ur, Corinth, Uz

ANSWERS:

1. Old (Ninth book of the Old Testament)
2. Gideon (Judges 6:13–15)
3. Fig (Genesis 3:7–8)
4. 300 (Judges 7:7–8)
5. Nun (Numbers 27:18)
6. Uz (Job 1:1)

Score Correct: _____ Date: _____ Name: _____
Study Notes: _____
_____
_____

Quiz 103

1. Is the book of Oracle in the Old Testament, New Testament, or neither?
2. What does Jesus tell the Pharisees it is lawful to do on the Sabbath?
   Tend to sick, Pray out loud, Feast together, Do well
3. From John 3, who was a Pharisee and a ruler among the Jews?
   Nicodemus, Annas, Caiaphas, Gamaliel
4. Who built the original house (temple) of the Lord in Jerusalem?
   Isaac, Abraham, Samuel, Solomon
5. What did Saul use a couple of times in attempts to kill David?
   Poison, Javelin, Mallet, Sling
6. Who was the mother of Gad and Asher?
   Jezebel, Anna, Rachel, Zilpah

ANSWERS:

1. Neither (Divine utterance of guidance delivered to humans through an intermediary)
2. Do well (Matthew 12:1–2, 12)
3. Nicodemus (John 3:1)
4. Solomon (1 Chronicles 28:9–13)
5. Javelin (1 Samuel 18:11, 1 Samuel 19:10)
6. Zilpah (Genesis 35:26)

Score Correct: _____ Date: _____ Name: _____
Study Notes: _____
_____
_____

Quiz 104

1. Is the book of Leviticus in the Old Testament, New Testament, or neither?
2. As Absalom rode upon a mule, his head and hair became tangled in and hung under the thick boughs of?
   Burning bush, Mighty cypress, Briars and thickets, Great oak
3. On being old and stricken in years, what did King David's servants bring to him to keep him warm?
   Hot bricks, Young virgin, Canopy skins, Wool from finest sheep
4. Whose last words were, "Turn thine hand, and carry me out of the host; for I am wounded"?
   Paul, John the Baptist, Ahab, Job
5. From Proverbs, which king was taught prophecy by his mother?
   Lemuel, Neco, Ben-Hadad, Jehu
6. Who was the father of Gideon?
   Job, Jeremiah, Josiah, Joash

ANSWERS:

1. Old (Third book of the Old Testament)
2. Great oak (2 Samuel 18:9–10)
3. Young virgin (1 Kings 1:1–3)
4. Ahab (1 Kings 22:20, 34–35)
5. Lemuel (Proverbs 31:1)
6. Joash (Judges 7:14)

Score Correct: _____ Date: _____ Name: _____
Study Notes: _____
_____
_____

Quiz 105

1. Is the book of 1 Chronicles in the Old Testament, New Testament, or neither?
2. Whose last words were, "God will surely visit you, and ye shall carry up my bones from hence"?
    Moses, Noah, Joseph, Adam
3. Which book recounts the story of the Israelites wandering in the desert for forty years?
    Genesis, Hebrews, James, Romans
4. Why did David meet Goliath without armor?
    Faith in God, Not proved it (not used to it), Too poor to buy, Size not handy
5. Where were many men slain for looking into the Ark of the Covenant?
    Succoth, Troas, Sychar, Bethshemesh
6. What sorcerer in Samaria became a believer?
    Hiel, Simon, Rehoboam, Omri

ANSWERS:

1. Old (Thirteenth book of the Old Testament)
2. Joseph (Genesis 50:25–26)
3. Hebrews (Hebrews 3:16–17)
4. Not proved it (not used to it) (1 Samuel 17:38–40)
5. Bethshemesh (1 Samuel 6:19)
6. Simon (Acts 8:5, 9, 13)

Score Correct: _____ Date: _____ Name: _____
Study Notes: _____
_____
_____

Quiz 106

1. Is the book of Kedemah in the Old Testament, New Testament, or neither?
2. What was the Lord's answer when Peter asked, "How oft shall my brother sin against me, and I forgive him"?
   Once, Thrice, Seven, Seventy times seven
3. In Matthew, how many Beatitudes from Jesus's Sermon on the Mount begin with "Blessed are"?
   6, 7, 8, 9
4. Near what city was Saul traveling when he heard the voice of Jesus?
   Antioch, Damascus, Paphos, Rome
5. Which tribe of Israel was set apart to serve in the Holy Temple?
   Dan, Gad, Levi, Simeon
6. Which of these men appeared the earliest in scripture?
   Moses, Jacob, Samuel, Abraham

ANSWERS:

1. Neither (A son of Ishmael and the tribe's name he headed)
2. Seventy times seven (Matthew 18:21–22)
3. 9 (Matthew 5:3–11)
4. Damascus (Acts 9:1–4)
5. Levi (Numbers 8:14–15)
6. Abraham (Genesis 17)

Score Correct: _____ Date: _____ Name: _____
Study Notes: _____
_____
_____

Quiz 107

1. Is the book of Ninevites in the Old Testament, New Testament, or neither?
2. Whose lyre-playing with his hand caused Saul's "evil spirit" to leave him?
    Solomon, Alexander, David, Haman
3. Esau sold his birthright for a mess of bread and _____ of lentiles?
    Gold, Pottage, Oil, Manna
4. Where was the burial place of Samuel?
    Gilgal, Joppa, Corinth, Ramah
5. Who was the firstborn of Hezron's three sons?
    Ram, Chelubai, Jerahmeel, Bunah
6. Jebus is another name for . . . ?
    Jericho, Jerusalem, Judah, Joshua

ANSWERS:

1. Neither (Inhabitants of Nineveh)
2. David (1 Samuel 16:23)
3. Pottage (Genesis 25:33–34)
4. Ramah (1Samuel 25:1, 28:3)
5. Jerahmeel (1 Chronicles 2:9)
6. Jerusalem (Judges 19:10)

Score Correct: _____ Date: _____ Name: _____
Study Notes: _____
_____
_____

Quiz 108

1. Is the book of 1 Corinthians in the Old Testament, New Testament, or neither?
2. Which city was the second of the seven churches in Asia mentioned by John in Revelation?
   Derbe, Gomorrah, Beersheba, Smyrna
3. What rich man of Arimathaea owned the tomb where Jesus was buried?
   Joseph, Barabbas, Nathaniel, Asher
4. From 1 Corinthians 16, "Let all your things be done with _____."
   Understanding, Hope, Friendship, Charity
5. What prophet came from among the herdmen of Tekoa?
   Joel, Hosea, Daniel, Amos
6. From Acts 8, what magician came to be baptized by Philip?
   Balaam, Endor, Simon, Laban

ANSWERS:
1. New (Seventh book of the New Testament)
2. Smyrna (Revelation 1:11)
3. Joseph (Matthew 27:57–60)
4. Charity (1 Corinthians 16:14)
5. Amos (Amos 1:1)
6. Simon (Acts 8:9, 13)

Score Correct: _____ Date: _____ Name: _____
Study Notes: _____

_____

_____

Quiz 109

1. Is the book of Gether in the Old Testament, New Testament, or neither?
2. When the seventh seal was opened, there was silence in heaven for about . . . ?
    One breath, Half an hour, Full day, Three days
3. Who was king of Persia when Daniel had his vision of a man clothed in linen?
    Darius, Xerxes, Artaxerxes, Cyrus
4. In 1 Chronicles, which descendant of Caleb was called the Garmite?
    Keilah, Amnon, Rinnah, Benhanan
5. What region with the meaning of ten cities was a location of Jesus's ministry?
    Pentateuch, Trinidad, Lilliom, Decapolis
6. From 1 Kings 19, how many days and nights did Elijah fast?
    7, 21, 40, 70

ANSWERS:

1. Neither (Aram's son and grandson of Shem)
2. Half an hour (Revelation 8:1)
3. Cyrus (Daniel 10:1, 5–7)
4. Keilah (1 Chronicles 4:19)
5. Decapolis (Matthew 4:25)
6. 40 (1 Kings 19:2, 7–8)

Score Correct: _____ Date: _____ Name: _____
Study Notes: _____
_____
_____

Quiz 110

1. Is the book of Exodus in the Old Testament, New Testament, or neither?
2. What part of David's mighty men could run as swift as the roes (gazelles) upon the mountains?
   Revlons, Gadites, Madaites, Henochs
3. From 1 Kings 20, how many kings came with Benhadad against King Ahab?
   2, 4, 7, 32
4. Which has three books, as in first (1), second (2), and third (3)?
   Peter, Thessalonians, John, Corinthians
5. From Judges 20, what tribe had seven hundred left-handed men?
   Benjamites, Samarians, Pharisees, Sadducees
6. Which priest took the first census of the Hebrews?
   Eleazar, Melchizedek, Ehud, Jabin

ANSWERS:

1. Old (Second book of the Old Testament)
2. Gadites (1 Chronicles 12:8)
3. 32 (1 Kings 20:2, 16)
4. John (1 John, 2 John, 3 John)
5. Benjamites (Judges 20:15–16)
6. Eleazer (Numbers 26:1–2)

Score Correct: _____ Date: _____ Name: _____
Study Notes: _____
_____
_____

Quiz 111

1. Is the book of 3 John in the Old Testament, New Testament, or neither?
2. Which woman was chosen to be queen through a beauty pageant, destined to reign for the rest of her life?
   Bathsheba, Tahpenes, Jezebel, Esther
3. Paul described what devout woman as "our sister"?
   Rachel, Deborah, Martha, Phoebe
4. Muppim, Huppim, and Ard were all whose younger sons?
   Gabriel, Michael, Benjamin, Paul
5. Where was the longest epistle of Paul sent?
   Rome, Joppa, Gibeon, Nazareth
6. In Genesis, who/what told the first-ever lie?
   Adam, Eve, Serpent, Cain

ANSWERS:

1. New (Twenty-fifth book of the New Testament)
2. Esther (Esther 2:3–4, 7–8, 15–16)
3. Phoebe (Romans 16:1–2)
4. Benjamin (Genesis 46:21)
5. Rome (Romans, Sixth book of New Testament and longest of the 13 Pauline epistles)
6. Serpent (Genesis 3:4)

Score Correct: _____ Date: _____ Name: _____
Study Notes: _____
_____
_____

Quiz 112

1. Is the book of Miriam in the Old Testament, New Testament, or neither?
2. From Leviticus 24's rules for restitution, what other body part is mentioned besides "eye for eye"?
   Nose, Tooth, Finger, Toe
3. The Lord sent Jeremiah to the house of what type of tradesman?
   Carpenter, Shopkeeper, Tailor, Potter
4. In Acts 5, how were the apostles released from prison?
   Broke out, Walls caved, Freed by an angel, Guard gave key
5. From Acts 8, Candace was queen of the. . .?
   Israelites, Ethiopians, Gadites, Ephesians
6. Which book follows Ruth?
   1 Samuel, Esther, Daniel, Amos

ANSWERS:

1. Neither (Prophetess sister of Aaron and Moses)
2. Tooth (Leviticus 24:20)
3. Potter (Jeremiah 18:1–2)
4. Freed by an angel (Acts 5:17–20)
5. Ethiopians (Acts 8:27)
6. 1 Samuel (Ninth book of the Old Testament)

Score Correct: _____ Date: _____ Name: _____
Study Notes: _____
_____
_____

Quiz 113

1. Is the book of Amos in the Old Testament, New Testament, or neither?
2. Who pondered to God, "Shall a child be born unto him that is an hundred years old"?
   Agrippa, Abraham, Adam, Aaron
3. From Acts 5, who convinced the Jerusalem council not to stone the apostles?
   Haggai, Shebna, Gamaliel, Levi
4. In 2 Corinthians, who does Paul describe as a "new creature"?
   The unborn, Innocent children, Commandment keepers, Any man in Christ
5. Besides Abiathar, who was a high priest during the reign of David?
   Passhur, Zadok, Caiaphas, Zebedee
6. How many days was Lazarus in the grave before being resurrected?
   3, 4, 7, 10

ANSWERS:
1. Old (Thirtieth book of the Old Testament)
2. Abraham (Genesis 17:17)
3. Gamaliel (Acts 5:26, 34–35)
4. Any man in Christ (2 Corinthians 5:17)
5. Zadok (2 Samuel 19:11)
6. 4 (John 11:14, 39)

Score Correct: _____ Date: _____ Name: _____
Study Notes: _____
_____
_____

Quiz 114

1. Is the book of Bela in the Old Testament, New Testament, or neither?
2. How many shekels of gold were plundered by the Israelites after the battle with the Midianites?
   512, 1200, 5042, 16750
3. From 2 Timothy, "All scripture is given by inspiration of God, and is profitable for _____."
   Living, Believers, Eternity, Doctrine
4. Which book mentions "the beginning of the creation of God"?
   No book does, Genesis, Ezekiel, Revelation
5. Hell is a place where what dieth not, and the fire is not quenched?
   Worm, Body, Soul, Greed
6. Who's the only woman with her age mentioned (at death)?
   Eve, Ruth, Leah, Sarah

ANSWERS:
1. Neither (City on the Dead Sea's shore, not far from Sodom)
2. 16750 (Numbers 31:3, 52)
3. Doctrine (2 Timothy 3:16)
4. Revelation (Revelation 3:14)
5. Worm (Mark 9:43–44)
6. Sarah (Genesis 23:1–2)

Score Correct: _____ Date: _____ Name: _____
Study Notes: _____
_____
_____

Quiz 115

1. Is the book of Myra in the Old Testament, New Testament, or neither?
2. From 2 Chronicles 26, at what age did Uzziah become king of Jerusalem?
   16, 30, 65, 99
3. Who did the Lord ask, "Why is thy countenance fallen"?
   Eve, Ahaz, Cain, Esau
4. According to Paul, it is better to marry than to do what with passion?
   Lust, Serve, Burn, Speak
5. In the book of Exodus, who/what saw the back of God?
   Adam, The serpent, Abraham, Moses
6. What did Methuselah become at 187 years old?
   Saved, Invalid, Father, Martyr

ANSWERS:

1. Neither (One of the chief towns of Lycia known for its rock-cut tombs in modern day SW Turkey)
2. 16 (2 Chronicles 26:3)
3. Cain (Genesis 4:6)
4. Burn (1 Corinthians 7:9)
5. Moses (Exodus 33:17, 23)
6. Father (Genesis 5:25)

Score Correct: _____ Date: _____ Name: _____
Study Notes: _____
_____
_____

Quiz 116

1. Is the book of Ozem in the Old Testament, New Testament, or neither?
2. Along with scribes, who else did Jesus accuse of devouring widows' houses?
   Sadducees, Midianites, Israelites, Pharisees
3. Which book contains the only three scripture verses that mention God laughing?
   Psalms, Proverbs, Song of Solomon, Titus
4. For how many days did Goliath take his stand for a man to fight him?
   2, 6, 10, 40
5. In Genesis, who did God ask, "Is any thing too hard for the Lord"?
   Moses, Adam, Noah, Abraham
6. How many loaves of bread were used to feed the five thousand?
   2, 3, 4, 5

ANSWERS:

1. Neither (Sixth son of Jesse)
2. Pharisees (Matthew 23:13–14)
3. Psalms (Psalms 2:4, 37:13, 59:8)
4. 40 (1 Samuel 17:4, 16)
5. Abraham (Genesis 18:13–14)
6. 5 (Matthew 14:19–21)

Score Correct: _____ Date: _____ Name: _____
Study Notes: _____
_____
_____

Quiz 117

1. Is the book of 2 Corinthians in the Old Testament, New Testament, or neither?
2. Foolishness is bound in the heart of a child; but what shall drive it far from him?
   Broken dream, Rod of correction, Stern father, Evil sibling
3. From Isaiah 45, who did God ask, "Shall the clay say to him that fashioneth it"?
   Gideon, Peter, Cyrus, Elijah
4. In scripture, who was the first person to become drunken?
   Ham, Enoch, Cain, Noah
5. What Jewish ruler visited Jesus by night?
   Hezekiah, Barabbas, Nicodemus, Darius
6. Who of these was Moses's assistant?
   Joshua, Gad, Nun, Jethro

ANSWERS:

1. New (Eighth book of the New Testament)
2. Rod of correction (Proverbs 22:15)
3. Cyrus (Isaiah 45:1, 9)
4. Noah (Genesis 9:20–21)
5. Nicodemus (John 3:1–2)
6. Joshua (Exodus 24:13)

Score Correct: _____ Date: _____ Name: _____
Study Notes: _____

_____

_____

Quiz 118

1. Is the book of Tarshish in the Old Testament, New Testament, or neither?
2. Who took the horn of oil and anointed David in the midst of his brethren, as the Lord's spirit came upon him from that day forward?
   Solomon, Samuel, Isaac, Moses
3. After Eve, the first woman mentioned in scripture, who was the second listed or referenced to?
   Daughter of Adam, Adah, Cain's wife, Naaman
4. From Philippians, "I can do all things through Christ which _____ me."
   Strengtheneth, Fashioneth, Sowest, Favoreth
5. What do moth and rust destroy on earth but not in heaven?
   Gates, Treasures, Riches, Belts
6. Who was the brother of Moses?
   Chemosh, Aaron, Amram, Marduk

ANSWERS:

1. Neither (Phoenician port, perhaps in Spain)
2. Samuel (1 Samuel 16:13)
3. Cain's wife (Genesis 4:17)
4. Strengtheneth (Philippians 4:13)
5. Treasures (Matthew 6:19–20)
6. Aaron (Exodus 6:20)

Score Correct: _____ Date: _____ Name: _____
Study Notes: _____
_____
_____

Quiz 119

1. Is the book of Athaliah in the Old Testament, New Testament, or neither?
2. How many times is Messias or Messiah, which means "anointed," listed in scripture?
   4, 7, 15, 29
3. In Matthew 10, Jesus instructed the apostles to go among the lost sheep of the house of?
   Heathen, Gentiles, Galatia, Israel
4. Who was the only woman whose name was changed by God?
   Gomer, Lo-ruhamah, Huzzab, Sarai
5. What was the name of Seth's son, thus Adam's grandson?
   Eliam, Eadbhard, Enos, Eadmer
6. Noah's Ark came to rest upon the mountains of . . . ?
   Sinai, Zion, Ararat, Ebal

ANSWERS:

1. Neither (Wife of King Jehoram of Judah)
2. 4 (John 1:41, 4:25, Daniel 9:25–26)
3. Israel (Matthew 10:5–6)
4. Sarai (To Sarah) (Genesis 17:15)
5. Enos (Genesis 4:26)
6. Ararat (Genesis 8:4)

Score Correct: _____ Date: _____ Name: _____
Study Notes: _____
_____
_____

Quiz 120

1. Is the book of Parmashta in the Old Testament, New Testament, or neither?
2. Scripture's first dream came to Abimelech warning him to release what woman from his harem?
   Eve, Adah, Naamah, Sarah
3. What "queen of" came to visit Solomon to prove (test) him with hard questions?
   Sheba, Pharaoh, Persia, Judah
4. What happened to Moses's rod when he cast it on the ground?
   Broke in two, Spoke to him, Became a serpent, Blazed up
5. How many books of the Bible begin with the letter "H"?
   1, 2, 3, 4
6. What godly son was born to Hannah and Elkanah in answer to prayer?
   Ezekiel, Paul, Samuel, Hosea

ANSWERS:
1. Neither (A son of Haman slain in Shushan)
2. Sarah (Genesis 20:2–3)
3. Sheba (1 Kings 10:1)
4. Became a serpent (Exodus 4:1–4)
5. 4 (Habakkuk, Haggai, Hebrews, Hosea)
6. Samuel (1 Samuel 1:9–10, 20–21)

Score Correct: _____ Date: _____ Name: _____
Study Notes: _____
_____
_____

Queen of Sheba comes to see Solomon's wisdom
Courtesy of: clipart.christiansunite.com

Quiz 121

1. Is the book of Barabbas in the Old Testament, New Testament, or neither?
2. Jesus said, "I must work the works of him that sent me, while it is day: the _____ cometh, when no man can work."
   Winds, Night, Rains, Brimstone
3. How many times do the words "chicken" or "chickens" appear in scripture?
   1, 16, 29, 84
4. Be ready for the coming of Christ for judgment and to do what without ceasing?
   Look to the heavens, Pray, Cry for forgiveness, Witness
5. At the end of Acts, where in Rome did Paul dwell two whole years?
   Temple, King's palace, Mountainside tent, His own hired house
6. From Judges 14, what young animal took Samson by surprise attack?
   Bear, Fox, Lion, Boar

ANSWERS:

1. Neither (Prisoner chosen over Jesus Christ to be released by Pontius Pilate)
2. Night (John 9:4)
3. 1 (Matthew 23:37)
4. Pray (1 Thessalonians 5:2, 17)
5. Hired (rented) house (Acts 28:30)
6. Lion (Judges 14:5–6)

Score Correct: _____ Date: _____ Name: _____
Study Notes: _____
_____
_____

Quiz 122

1. Is the book of Zaza in the Old Testament, New Testament, or neither?
2. In the sight of elders of Israel, where did Moses smite the rock that produced water his people needed?
   Pisgah, Sinai, Gilboa, Horeb
3. What did God write His commandments on?
   Pillars of smoke, Linen parchments, Holy ground, Tables of stone
4. Which was not a biblical nationality in scripture?
   Amorites, Woolites, Perizzites, Canaanites
5. From Ephesians, "One Lord, one faith, one _____."
   Heaven, Baptism, Salvation, Witness
6. Who was a certain Jew, born at Alexandria, and mighty in the scriptures?
   Apollos, Jupiter, Barnabas, Mercurius

ANSWERS:

1. Neither (One of the sons of Jonathan)
2. Horeb (Exodus 17:5–6)
3. Tables of stone (Exodus 24:12, 31:18)
4. Woolites (Joshua 24:11)
5. Baptism (Ephesians 4:5)
6. Apollos (Acts 18:24)

Score Correct: _____ Date: _____ Name: _____
Study Notes: _____
_____
_____

Quiz 123

1. Is the book of Hebrews in the Old Testament, New Testament, or neither?
2. When bringing their sacrificial animals as peace offerings to the Lord, the Israelites were told to give what part to the priest as a gift?
   Breast, All feet, Drumstick, Right shoulder
3. Who did the Lord call a third time, after which the person answered, "Speak; for thy servant heareth"?
   Isaac, Samuel, Moses, Elijah
4. From Proverbs, "In all thy ways acknowledge him, and he shall _____ thy paths."
   Fulfill, Join, Direct, Journey
5. Who said, "Behold, I am at the point to die: and what profit shall this birthright do to me"?
   Cain, Abel, Esau, Jacob
6. Where was the scene of the burning bush that Moses encountered?
   Mount Horeb, Jacob's ladder, Dhiban village, River Jordan

ANSWERS:

1. New (Nineteenth book of the New Testament)
2. Right shoulder (Leviticus 7:29–32)
3. Samuel (1 Samuel 3:8–10)
4. Direct (Proverbs 3:6)
5. Esau (Genesis 25:32)
6. Mount Horeb (Exodus 3:1–2)

Score Correct: _____ Date: _____ Name: _____
Study Notes: _____
_____
_____

Quiz 124

1. Is the book of 2 Peter in the Old Testament, New Testament, or neither?
2. Where did Paul leave Titus, one of his converts of a common faith?
    Cyprus, Crete, Melita, Michmas
3. What was the occupation of Demetrius, who denounced Paul?
    Carpenter, Shepherd, Silversmith, Tentmaker
4. "Blessed are they that mourn; for they shall be _____."
    Glorified, Lifted, Praised, Comforted
5. From 2 Chronicles, what did Solomon ask for?
    Wealth, Long life, Wisdom, Honor
6. Who saw living angelic beings with wheels?
    Elijah, Jeremiah, Darius, Ezekiel

ANSWERS:

1. New (Twenty-second book of the New Testament)
2. Crete (Titus 1:1–5)
3. Silversmith (Acts 19:24–26)
4. Comforted (Matthew 5:4)
5. Wisdom (2 Chronicles 1:11)
6. Ezekiel (Ezekiel 1:15–21)

Score Correct: _____ Date: _____ Name: _____
Study Notes: _____

_____

_____

Quiz 125

1. Is the book of Lamentations in the Old Testament, New Testament, or neither?
2. From Mark 10, "For even the Son of man came not to be ministered unto, but to minister, and to give his life a _____ for many."
   Testament, Ransom, Lifeboat, Sanctuary
3. Who told Queen Esther, who had been given a position of power, that she had come to the kingdom for such a time as this?
   Hatach, Mordecai, Ahasuerus, Haman
4. Obadiah, one of the minor prophets, announced judgment on what nation for its sins against Judah and Jerusalem?
   Edom, Ethiopia, Egypt, Libya
5. In 1 Kings, who did Ahab call the one that troubleth Israel?
   Obadiah, Elijah, Omri, Ehud
6. Chebar is best described as a(n) . . . ?
   Evil force, Shield of faith, Weapon of war, River

ANSWERS:
1. Old (Twenty-fifth book of the Old Testament)
2. Ransom (Mark 10:45)
3. Mordecai (Esther 4:13–14)
4. Edom (Obadiah 1:1, 8)
5. Elijah (1 Kings 18:17–18)
6. River (Ezekiel 1:1)

Score Correct: _____ Date: _____ Name: _____
Study Notes: _____
_____
_____

Quiz 126

1. Is the book of Tarsus in the Old Testament, New Testament, or neither?
2. What is the shortest book in the New Testament when counting the number of words in Hebrew or Greek?
   Titus, 3 John, Jude, Revelation
3. The harlot Rahab hid two spies from the king of Jericho's men on the roof with . . . ?
   Ears of corn, Stalks of flax, Weeds of the hill, Rocks from the pond
4. Which of Israel's enemy kingdoms did Sennacherib rule over as king?
   Moab, Assyria, Edom, Babylon
5. The Lord Jesus said, "It is more _____ to give than to receive."
   Compassionate, Blessed, Goodness, Delightful
6. From Hebrews, what should we approach boldly unto in time of need?
   Death, Temple leadership, Confessions, Throne of grace

ANSWERS:
1. Neither (Chief city of Cilicia located in today's province of Mersin, Turkey)
2. 3 John (219 words), also shortest in entire Bible
3. Stalks of flax (Joshua 2:1–6)
4. Assyria (Isaiah 36:1)
5. Blessed (Acts 20:35)
6. Throne of grace (Hebrews 4:16)

Score Correct: _____ Date: _____ Name: _____
Study Notes: _____
_____
_____

Quiz 127

1. Is the book of Thyatira in the Old Testament, New Testament, or neither?
2. Who took Paul's girdle (belt) and bound his hands and feet when he came unto Caesarea on his journey to Jerusalem?
   Agabus, Demas, Elidad, Jesher
3. What was the name of King Ahasuerus's evil advisor who convinced him to persecute the Jews?
   Elam, Haman, Jorim, Manaen
4. Who was the grandson of Saul and the lame son of Jonathan?
   Micri, Mephibosheth, Maaseiah, Magpiash
5. Sarah died in Kirjatharba at what age?
   19, 88, 127, 200
6. Who was the father of Joshua?
   Meshech, Nun, Ozni, Gaal

ANSWERS:

1. Thyatira (One of Seven Churches of Revelation, aka the Seven Churches of the Apocalypse)
2. Agabus (Acts 21:8–12)
3. Haman (Esther 3:8, 12)
4. Mephibosheth (2 Samuel 4:4)
5. 127 (Genesis 23:1–2)
6. Nun (Exodus 33:11)

Score Correct: _____ Date: _____ Name: _____
Study Notes: _____
_____
_____

Quiz 128

1. Is the book of Korah in the Old Testament, New Testament, or neither?
2. Uzziah was sixteen years old when he became the king of Jerusalem, and he reigned for how many years?
   3, 25, 46, 52
3. What book's first verse is, "How doth the city sit solitary, that was full of people"?
   Judges, Ruth, Ezra, Lamentations
4. Where was Paul mistaken for Mercurius because he was the chief speaker?
   Antioch, Perga, Gibeon, Lystra
5. Who said, "Naked came I out of my mother's womb, and naked shall I return thither"?
   Cain, Moses, Job, Hattil
6. From Hebrews 7, what priest was without mother or father?
   Jehoiada, Melchisedec, Eleazar, Leviticus

ANSWERS:

1. Neither (Third son of Esau by Aholibamah)
2. 52 (2 Chronicles 26:3)
3. Lamentations (Lamentations 1:1)
4. Lystra (Acts 14:8–12)
5. Job (Job 1:21)
6. Melchisedec (Hebrews 7:1–3)

Score Correct: _____ Date: _____ Name: _____
Study Notes: _____
_____
_____

Quiz 129

1. Is the book of Othniel in the Old Testament, New Testament, or neither?
2. Who sent word to Pontius Pilate to leave Christ alone after having a dream about Him?
   Wounded soldier, Trustworthy servant, High priest, Pilate's wife
3. Put these in order starting with the longest living, the second longest, third, and fourth?
   Adam, Jared, Methuselah, Noah
4. What descendant of Cain was considered the father and inventor of tents?
   Gaal, Jabal, Abel, Adam
5. Hosea's third child was a son called Loammi, a name meaning . . . ?
   Peacemaker, Not my people, Courage, Of the swamp
6. Who did the Lord tell to tear down all pagan altars?
   Elihu, Moses, Methuselah, Carpus

ANSWERS:

1. Neither (Israel judge, younger brother of Caleb)
2. Pilate's wife (Matthew 27:17–19)
3. Methuselah 969 (Genesis 5:27), Jared 962 (Genesis 5:20, Noah 950 (Genesis 9:29), Adam 930 (Genesis 5:5)
4. Jabal (Genesis 4:20)
5. Not my people (Hosea 1:8–9)
6. Moses (Exodus 34:8, 12–13)

Score Correct: _____ Date: _____ Name: _____
Study Notes: _____
_____
_____

Quiz 130

1. Is the book of Cyrus in the Old Testament, New Testament, or neither?
2. What did the captain of the host of the Lord who met Joshua outside Jericho tell him to remove?
   Belt, Cloak, Guilt, Shoes
3. Cherith, Eshcol, and Zered are specifically referred to as . . . ?
   Mountains, Camels, Inns, Brooks
4. From 2 Samuel, who was commander of David's army?
   Amasa, Joab, Joshua, Julius
5. Who/what was Caesarea Philippi?
   Julius Caesar's wife, Towns, Tomb, Mountain
6. From Luke 3, how old was Jesus at His baptism?
   A baby, 7, 12, Around 30

ANSWERS:
1. Neither (Persia king 559–530 BC)
2. Shoes (Joshua 5:13–15)
3. Brooks (1 Kings 17:3, Numbers 13:23, Deuteronomy 2:13)
4. Joab (2 Samuel 8:14–16)
5. Towns (Located in the foothills of Mt. Hermon) (Mark 8:27)
6. Around 30 (Luke 3:21–23)

Score Correct: _____ Date: _____ Name: _____
Study Notes: _____
_____
_____

Quiz 131

1. Is the book of Ethan in the Old Testament, New Testament, or neither?
2. Who took Ijon, Abelbethmaachah, Janoah, Kedesh, Hazor, Gilead, and Galilee and carried them captive to Assyria?
   Tiglathpileser, Tabrimmon, Vaizatha, Zebina
3. To whom was the Lord talking when He said, "Two nations are in thy womb," as the children struggled together within her?
   Rebekah, Sarah, Ruth, Deborah
4. On wrestling with a mysterious man, who said, "I will not let thee go, except thou bless me"?
   Ashhur, Jacob, Carshena, Jalam
5. Who told his brothers about a dream, and it annoyed them to hatred?
   Ishmael, Joseph, Benjamin, Haran
6. From Romans, what does Paul say is the fulfillment of the law?
   Obedience, Submission, Faith, Love

ANSWERS:

1. Neither (Boy at King David's court well known for his wisdom)
2. Tiglathpileser (2 Kings 15:29)
3. Rebekah (Genesis 25:20–23)
4. Jacob (Genesis 32:24–27)
5. Joseph (Genesis 37:5)
6. Love (Romans 13:10)

Score Correct: _____ Date: _____ Name: _____
Study Notes: _____
_____
_____

Quiz 132

1. Is the book of Bariah in the Old Testament, New Testament, or neither?

2. Paul said, "For there is no difference between the Jew and the _____: for the same Lord over all is rich unto all that call upon him."
   Gentile, Foreigners, Greek, Syrians

3. Where didn't King Ahaz sacrifice and burn incense?
   In the high places, Behind large rocks, On the hills, Under every green tree

4. What does the sorrow of the world worketh?
   Hell's gate, Anger, Antichrist, Death

5. Where did Abraham bury his wife Sarah, in the cave of the field of?
   Makkedah, Adullam, Machpelah, Zoar

6. Which was known as the city of palm trees?
   Jericho, Damascus, Betah, Gath

ANSWERS:

1. Neither (Descendant of David in the line of Solomon)
2. Greek (Romans 10:12)
3. Behind large rocks (2 Kings 16:2–4)
4. Death (2 Corinthians 7:10)
5. Machpelah (Genesis 23:19)
6. Jericho (Deuteronomy 34:3)

Score Correct: _____ Date: _____ Name: _____
Study Notes: _____
_____
_____

Quiz 133

1. Is the book of Hebron in the Old Testament, New Testament, or neither?
2. According to Paul in Galatians, where is the site of Mount Sinai?
   Egypt, Arabia, Greece, Edom
3. Who had a residence in Derbe and was one of Paul's seven traveling companions?
   Timothy, Aeneas, Gaius, Ananias
4. In John 19, who said, "What I have written, I have written"?
   Daniel, John the Baptist, Pilate, Jesus
5. About how old was the widowed prophetess, Anna, when she saw the young Jesus in the temple?
   60, 84, 95, 102
6. From Matthew 7, upon what did the wise man build his house?
   Bush, Sand, Rock, Sea

ANSWERS:

1. Neither (City about midway between Jerusalem and Beersheba)
2. Arabia (Galatians 4:25)
3. Gaius (Acts 20:1–4)
4. Pilate (John 19:21–22)
5. 84 (Luke 2:36–38)
6. Rock (Matthew 7:24–25)

Score Correct: _____ Date: _____ Name: _____
Study Notes: _____
_____
_____

Quiz 134

1. Is the book of Acts in the Old Testament, New Testament, or neither?
2. Elias was a man subject to like passions as we are, and he prayed earnestly that it might not rain: and it rained not on the earth for how long?
   7 months, 1 year 4 months, 3 years 6 months, 7 years
3. What "holy" thing did Paul tell Timothy that men everywhere should lift up in prayer?
   Songs, Hands, Spirits, Hearts
4. Which place was known as the land of promise flowing with milk and honey?
   New Jerusalem, Canaan, Babylon, Nod
5. What does the goodness of God lead one to?
   Heaven, Repentance, Church, Discipleship
6. From Titus 3, why did God save us?
   Earthly love, Our sins, His mercy, Divine intervention

ANSWERS:

1. New (Fifth book of the New Testament)
2. 3 years 6 months (James 5:17)
3. Hands (1 Timothy 2:8)
4. Canaan (Exodus 3:17)
5. Repentance (Romans 2:4)
6. His mercy (Titus 3:5)

Score Correct: _____ Date: _____ Name: _____
Study Notes: _____
_____
_____

Quiz 135

1. Is the book of Proverbs in the Old Testament, New Testament, or neither?
2. Fill in the blanks with the same word, "And if Christ be not risen, then is our preaching _____, and your faith is also _____."
   Useless, Repetitive, Brilliant, Vain
3. What did Paul say long hair is to a woman, for her hair is given her for a covering?
   Warmth, Forgiveness, Glory, Flowing
4. Along with all in the household, who was spared during the fall of Jericho?
   Deborah, Miriam, Abigail, Rahab
5. The River Nile was turned to what during the ten plagues of Egypt?
   Salt, Molten lava, Blood, Sheep urine
6. Who made the golden molten calf that the Israelites worshipped?
   Aaron, Moses, Enoch, Abraham

ANSWERS:

1. Old (Twentieth book of the Old Testament)
2. Vain (1 Corinthians 15:14)
3. Glory (1 Corinthians 11:15)
4. Rahab (Joshua 6:23–25)
5. Blood (Exodus 7:17-18)
6. Aaron (Exodus 32:1–4)

Score Correct: _____ Date: _____ Name: _____
Study Notes: _____
_____
_____

Quiz 136

1. Is the book of Ezra in the Old Testament, New Testament, or neither?
2. From 1 Peter, "Sanctify the Lord God in your hearts: and be ready always to give an answer to every man that asketh you a reason of the _____ that is in you."
   Love, Hope, Lord, Church
3. Which spy, as an inheritance, was awarded Hebron, a piece of Canaan?
   Gaddi, Ammiel, Sethur, Caleb
4. The phrase "to rob Peter to pay Paul" is found where in the Bible?
   Nowhere, Hebrews 12:1, James 1:27, Acts 16:31
5. The city of Bethel was originally called . . . ?
   Kirjath-sannah, Luz, Aphek, Japho
6. Jael was the wife of . . . ?
   John the Baptist, Heber the Kenite, Amaziah of Judah, Doeg the Edomite

ANSWERS:

1. Old (Fifteenth book of the Old Testament)
2. Hope (1 Peter 3:15)
3. Caleb (Joshua 14:6–7, 13–14)
4. Nowhere (Not found in Bible)
5. Luz (Genesis 28:19)
6. Heber the Kenite (Judges 4:17)

Score Correct: _____ Date: _____ Name: _____
Study Notes: _____
_____
_____

Quiz 137

1. Is the book of Hamuel in the Old Testament, New Testament, or neither?
2. Fill in the blank from Revelation, "Blessed is he that _____, and they that hear the words of this prophecy."
   Listens, Wonders, Cries, Readeth
3. Who commanded his servants to kill Amnon, son of David, when he was merry with wine?
   Kileab, Shimon, Absalom, Shephatiah
4. From Galatians 5, the fruit of the Spirit is made up of how many traits?
   3, 4, 9, 12
5. Ziph, Ziphah, Tiria, and Asareel were the sons of . . . ?
   Menahem, Jehaleleel, Elidad, Mattithiah
6. Whose wife said to her husband, "Curse God, and die"?
   Job, Solomon, Isaac, Herod

ANSWERS:

1. Neither (Son of Mishma, a Simeonite)
2. Readeth (Revelation 1:3)
3. Absalom (2 Samuel 13:28–29)
4. 9 (Galatians 5:22–23)
5. Jehaleleel (1 Chronicles 4:16)
6. Job (Job 2:9)

Score Correct: _____ Date: _____ Name: _____
Study Notes: _____
_____
_____

Quiz 138

1. Is the book of Jabal in the Old Testament, New Testament, or neither?
2. The Lord told Elijah to hide by which brook from which the ravens would feed him?
   Jordan, Salty, Ahava, Cherith
3. Ezra 7:21 is a unique verse in that it contains, lists, or says . . . ?
   Lord crying, Every letter of alphabet except one, Unforgiven sins, Antichrist identity
4. What did Jesus tell the multitudes were numbered?
   Days on earth, Hairs of their head, True friends, Enemies hurt
5. In Deuteronomy 34, Moses saw the promised land from what mountain?
   Hermon, Zion, Ararat, Nebo
6. Where did the harlot Rahab live in her house?
   Jericho, Philadelphia, Smyrna, Tarsus

ANSWERS:

1. Neither (Descendant of Cain and son of Lamech and Adah)
2. Cherith (1 Kings 17:1–4)
3. Every letter of alphabet except one (J)
4. Hairs of their head (Matthew 10:30, Luke 12:7)
5. Nebo (Deuteronomy 34:1–4)
6. Jericho (Joshua 2:1)

Score Correct: _____ Date: _____ Name: _____
Study Notes: _____
_____
_____

Quiz 139

1. Is the book of 2 Chronicles in the Old Testament, New Testament, or neither?
2. "Harlot," including harlot's, harlots, and harlots', is listed fifty times in scripture, while the word "prostitute" is mentioned only . . . ?
    Once, Twice, 5 times, 7 times
3. From the first chapter of James. what kind of man is like the waves of the sea, one that . . . ?
    Repents, Wavereth, Envies, Sleeps
4. How often did Absalom cut his hair, as it became too heavy to carry around?
    Daily, Weekly, Monthly, Yearly
5. Which apostle of Jesus was a publican (tax collector)?
    Andrew, John, James, Matthew
6. From what church was Silas?
    Unity, Bethany, Antioch, Trinity

ANSWERS:

1. Old (Fourteenth book of the Old Testament)
2. Once (Leviticus 19:29)
3. Wavereth (Doubts) (James 1:6)
4. Yearly (2 Samuel 14:25–26)
5. Matthew (Matthew 10:3)
6. Antioch (Acts 15:22)

Score Correct: _____ Date: _____ Name: _____
Study Notes: _____
_____
_____

Quiz 140

1. Is the book of Hyssop in the Old Testament, New Testament, or neither?
2. What bodily part(s) of Malchus, the high priest's servant, did Simon Peter cut off when he attempted to protect Jesus from being taken as a prisoner?
   Left thumb, Nose, Right ear, Both feet
3. The phrase "Holy One of Israel" is most often used in what book to describe the Lord?
   Genesis, Isaiah, Hosea, Revelation
4. From Psalms 141, "Let the righteous smite me; it shall be a _____."
   Judgment, Scorn, Grief, Kindness
5. What does the shield represent in the "armor of God"?
   Courage, Faith, Gallows, Doves
6. In John 6, Jesus said, "I am the _____ of life."
   Light, Wine, Giver, Bread

ANSWERS:

1. Neither (Shrub in the Lamiaceae or mint family)
2. Right ear (John 18:7–10)
3. Isaiah (In at least twenty-five verses)
4. Kindness (Psalms 141:5)
5. Faith (Ephesians 6:13, 16)
6. Bread (John 6:35)

Score Correct: _____ Date: _____ Name: _____
Study Notes: _____
_____
_____

Feeding the 5,000
Courtesy of: clipart.christiansunite.com

Quiz 141

1. Is the book of 2 Timothy in the Old Testament, New Testament, or neither?
2. Who did King Jehosophat appoint as the chief priest in all matters of the Lord?
   Asahel, Amariah, Eliasaph, Jesher
3. What relationship was Athaliah to King Ahaziah, who ruled Judah after Athaliah's death?
   Mother, Father, Sister, Brother
4. Who argued with the devil in a quarrel over the body of Moses?
   Michael the archangel, A beggar, Miriam, Zipporah
5. In John 10, Jesus said, "I am the good _____ ."
   Samaritan, Storyteller, Fisherman, Shepherd
6. Whose Egyptian handmaid was Hagar?
   Esther, Ruth, Sarai, Delilah

ANSWERS:

1. New (Sixteenth book of the New Testament)
2. Amariah (2 Chronicles 19:8, 11)
3. Mother (2 Chronicles 22:10–12)
4. Michael the archangel (Jude 1:9)
5. Shepherd (John 10:14)
6. Sarai (Genesis 16:1)

Score Correct: _____ Date: _____ Name: _____
Study Notes: _____
_____
_____

Quiz 142

1. Is the book of Jasper in the Old Testament, New Testament, or neither?
2. What was the name of the chiefest of the herdsmen that belonged to Saul?
   Doeg, Ram, Uzai, Peleg
3. From Zechariah 10, "For the idols have spoken _____."
   Hope, Vanity, Loudly, Nothing
4. What well was between Kadesh and Bered?
   Beerlahairoi, Baca, Bethlehem, Bahurim
5. Who built Elath and restored it to Judah?
   Solomon, Nimrod, Azariah, Hiel
6. Which book follows Acts?
   Romans, Mark, Ephesians, Colossians

ANSWERS:

1. Neither (One of the twelve gems inserted in the high priest's breastplate)
2. Doeg (1 Samuel 21:7)
3. Vanity (Zechariah 10:2)
4. Beerlahairoi (Genesis 16:14)
5. Azariah (2 Kings 14:21–22)
6. Romans (Sixth book of the New Testament)

Score Correct: _____ Date: _____ Name: _____
Study Notes: _____
_____
_____

Quiz 143

1. Is the book of David in the Old Testament, New Testament, or neither?
2. From 1 Timothy, what does the Holy Spirit say will happen to some in the latter times (last days)?
   Take their own life, Depart from the faith, Experience false miracles, Fall from grace
3. How many men did the Jews slay and destroy in the palace of Shushan on the first day of fighting?
   Fifty, One hundred, Five hundred, One thousand
4. To what creature robbed of her whelps (cubs) in the field did Hushai liken David?
   Dove, Fox, Bear, Snake
5. According to Paul, what should good ministers of Jesus Christ refuse and reject?
   Unclean meat, Old wives' fables, Unfounded gossip, False prophets
6. Under which rib was Abner, son of Ner, struck and slain by Joab?
   First, Third, Fourth, Fifth

ANSWERS:

1. Neither (Slayer of Goliath and later Israel's king)
2. Depart from the faith (1 Timothy 4:1)
3. Five hundred (Esther 9:5–6, 11 -12)
4. Bear (2 Samuel 17:1, 7–8)
5. Old wives' fables (1 Timothy 4:4–7)
6. Fifth (2 Samuel 3:25–27)

Score Correct: _____ Date: _____ Name: _____
Study Notes: _____
_____
_____

Quiz 144

1. Is the book of Revelation in the Old Testament, New Testament, or neither?
2. Which false prophet took off the yoke from the prophet Jeremiah's neck and broke it?
   Bar-Jesus, Jezebel, Hananiah, Zedekiah
3. Who did King Rehoboam love above all his wives and concubines?
   Mahalath, Jedidah, Maachah, Oholibamah
4. The Semites were descended from Shem, the son of _____?
   Moses, Noah, Paul, Jacob
5. From Luke 16. who was the last prophet before the arrival of Jesus?
   Obadiah, Jonah, Micah, John the Baptist
6. What shall come in the last days walking after their own lusts?
   Politicians, Scoffers, Fools, Serpents

ANSWERS:

1. New (Twenty-seventh and last book of the New Testament, also last book of the Bible)
2. Hananiah (Jeremiah 28:9–10)
3. Maachah (2 Chronicles 11:21)
4. Noah (Genesis 5:32)
5. John the Baptist (Luke 16:16)
6. Scoffers (2 Peter 3:3)

Score Correct: _____ Date: _____ Name: _____
Study Notes: _____
_____
_____

Quiz 145

1. Is the book of Elijah in the Old Testament, New Testament, or neither?
2. In Proverbs, the beauty of old men is the gray head, while the glory of young men is their . . . ?
   Imagination, Strength, Discretion, Instruction
3. Where was Paul stoned and left for dead?
   Miletus, Lystra, Kechries, Apollonia
4. From Genesis 2, what did God use to form man?
   Water, Dust, Robe, Wind
5. Which of Jesus's friends was buried in a cave?
   Mary, Martha, Lazarus, John the Baptist
6. What Phoenician city was home to Hiram?
   Endor, Patara, Tyre, Sardis

ANSWERS:

1. Neither (Prophet and miracle worker who lived in the northern kingdom of Israel)
2. Strength (Proverbs 20:29)
3. Lystra (Acts 14:6–8, 18–19)
4. Dust (Genesis 2:7)
5. Lazarus (John 11:1, 38)
6. Tyre (2 Samuel 5:11)

Score Correct: _____ Date: _____ Name: _____
Study Notes: _____
_____
_____

Quiz 146

1. Is the book of Heth in the Old Testament, New Testament, or neither?
2. Edar, Penuel, Shechem, and Lebanon are all mentioned as "what" in scripture?
    Wells, Brooks, Towers, Valleys
3. Under what kind of tree did Saul tarry in the uttermost part of Gibeah?
    Sycamore, Cedar, Apple, Pomegranate
4. What moved Noah to prepare the ark?
    Repentance, Lord's command, Stubbornness, An angel
5. Which prophet had a son named Shearjashub?
    Isaiah, Elijah, Nathan, Ahijah
6. What does the sorrow of the world worketh?
    Salvation, Truth, Anger, Death

ANSWERS:

1. Neither (Canaan descendant and Hittites ancestor)
2. Towers. Edar (Genesis 35:21), Penuel (Judges 8:17), Shechem (Judges 9:46), Lebanon (Song of Solomon 7:4)
3. Pomegranate (1 Samuel 14:2)
4. Lord's command (Genesis 6:13–14, 7:1, 5)
5. Isaiah (Isaiah 7:3)
6. Death (2 Corinthians 7:10)

Score Correct: _____ Date: _____ Name: _____
Study Notes: _____
_____
_____

Quiz 147

1. Is the book of Naomi in the Old Testament, New Testament, or neither?
2. What were the three men that Saul met at Tabor on the way to find his father's asses (donkeys) not carrying?
   Three kids, Bottle of wine, Three loaves of bread, Sack of barley
3. In Genesis 15, who was told to "look now toward heaven, and tell the stars"?
   Noah, Adam, Abram, Moses
4. What was the hometown village of Jeremiah, a biblical book author?
   Anathoth, Neapolis, Patara, Sodom
5. Who with his brethren sold their brother, Joseph, to a camel caravan?
   Cain, Judah, Silas, Joshua
6. Sisera was captain of the host of?
   Pharaoh, David, Hazor, Elishama

ANSWERS:
1. Neither (Wife of Elimelech, mother-in-law of Ruth)
2. Sack of barley (1 Samuel 10:1–3)
3. Abram (Genesis 15:3–5)
4. Anathoth (Jeremiah 1:1)
5. Judah (Genesis 37:23–27)
6. Hazor (1 Samuel 12:9)

Score Correct: _____ Date: _____ Name: _____

Study Notes: _____

_____

_____

Quiz 148

1. Is the book of Salmon in the Old Testament, New Testament, or neither?
2. What did the Philistines return to the Israelites along with a guilt offering of five golden emerods and five golden mice? Lachish Letters, Ark of the Lord, Dead Sea scrolls, Cypress timbers
3. Who was the daughter of King Jehoram who hid her nephew, young Joash, from being killed as a royal heir? Jehoshabeath, Aholibamah, Iscah, Mahalath
4. Abraham offered to sacrifice his only son Isaac on a mountaintop in the land of _____?
   Moriah, Ararat, Olives, Tabor
5. Naomi, the mother-in-law of Ruth, was married to whom? Ephriam, Elijah, Elimelech, Elisha
6. Where did Jacob and his family settle in Egypt? Armant, Goshen, Tehna, Dendera

ANSWERS:
1. Neither (Son of Nashon and a hill near Shechem)
2. Ark of the Lord (1 Samuel 6:1–4)
3. Jehoshabeath (2 Chronicles 22:11)
4. Moriah (Genesis 22:1–2)
5. Elimelech (Ruth 1:2)
6. Goshen (Genesis 47:1)

Score Correct: _____ Date: _____ Name: _____
Study Notes: _____
_____
_____

Quiz 149

1. Is the book of 1 Timothy in the Old Testament, New Testament, or neither?
2. From Proverbs, "Train up a child in the _____ he should go: and when he is old, he will not depart from it."
   Spirit, Way, Straight, Respect
3. Where did the Lord speak to Moses after they came out of the land of Egypt?
   Mount Carmel, Wilderness of Sinai, Sea of Galilee, Mount of Olives
4. What city does Zephaniah say will be forsaken and Ashkelon a desolation?
   Geba, Gaza, Golan, Gath
5. Who did Paul call "the beloved physician"?
   Mark, Luke, Artemas, John
6. What was the name of Cain's first child?
   Olad, Lizpha, Fosal, Enoch

ANSWERS:

1. New (Fifteenth book of the New Testament)
2. Way (Proverbs 22:6)
3. Wilderness of Sinai (Numbers 1:1)
4. Gaza (Zephaniah 2:4)
5. Luke (Colossians 4:14)
6. Enoch (Genesis 4:16–17)

Score Correct: _____ Date: _____ Name: _____
Study Notes: _____
_____
_____

Quiz 150

1. Is the book of Reba in the Old Testament, New Testament, or neither?
2. About how many beasts rising out of the sea did Daniel have a dream?
   4, 7, 13, 20
3. What did James say is a world of iniquity; and it is set on the fire of hell?
   Adulterer, Tongue, Ribald, Unfathered
4. Who was the first man in scripture to celebrate his birthday?
   Cain, Pharaoh, Enoch, Abraham
5. Which chapter in the book of Numbers is God's explanation of vows?
   1, 6, 10, 30
6. From Matthew 8, whose mother-in-law did Jesus heal?
   Elijah's, Solomon's, Daniel's, Peter's

ANSWERS:

1. Neither (One of the kings/dukes of Midian slain by the Israelites in the wilderness)
2. 4 (Daniel 7:1–3)
3. Tongue (James 3:6)
4. Pharaoh (Genesis 40:20)
5. 30 (Numbers 30:1–16)
6. Peter's (Matthew 8:14–15)

Score Correct: _____ Date: _____ Name: _____
Study Notes: _____
_____
_____

Quiz 151

1. Is the book of Corinth in the Old Testament, New Testament, or neither?
2. On the day of Pentecost, from where did the sound of a rushing mighty wind come?
   Heaven, Wavy sea, Mountaintops, Valley of Shaveh
3. According to Romans 11, whose loss meant "riches" for the Gentiles?
   Caesar, Lucifer, Israel, Syria
4. Who was the first to experience physical death?
   Adam, Abel, Aaron, Abraham
5. What book's last verse is, "Remember me, O my God, for good"?
   Malachi, Nehemiah, Hebrews, Revelation
6. Which apostle did Satan enter into?
   Judas, Thomas, James, Peter

ANSWERS:

1. Neither (Grecian city about forty-eight miles west of Athens)
2. Heaven (Acts 2:1–2)
3. Israel (Romans 11:7, 12)
4. Abel (Genesis 4:8)
5. Nehemiah (Nehemiah 13:31)
6. Judas (Luke 22:3)

Score Correct: _____ Date: _____ Name: _____
Study Notes: _____
_____
_____

Quiz 152

1. Is the book of Dinah in the Old Testament, New Testament, or neither?
2. King Solomon had his chariot trimmed in silver and gold, upholstered in purple, and made of what kind of wood?
   Lebanon, Gibeon, Manasseh, Ephraim
3. What scribe did Paul use in writing down the book of Romans that wrote his own greeting?
   Stephen, Benaiah, Cyrus, Tertius
4. Joel declared, "Beat your plowshares into swords, and your pruninghooks into . . ."?
   Hooks, Hammers, Dust, Spears
5. "Holy One of Israel" is most often used in which book to describe the Lord?
   Hosea, Revelation, Judges, Isaiah
6. From Genesis 35, who died giving birth to Benjamin?
   Rachel, Leah, Naomi, Ruth

ANSWERS:

1. Neither (Daughter of Jacob and Leah)
2. Lebanon (Song of Solomon 3:9–10)
3. Tertius (Romans 1:1, 16:22)
4. Spears (Joel 3:10)
5. Isaiah (At least twenty-five times)
6. Rachel (Genesis 35:16–20)

Score Correct: _____ Date: _____ Name: _____
Study Notes: _____
_____
_____

Quiz 153

1. Is the book of Philemon in the Old Testament, New Testament, or neither?
2. "All scripture is given by inspiration of God, and is profitable for doctrine, for reproof, for correction, for instruction in _____."
   Living, Battles, Redemption, Righteousness
3. What city was the fourth of the seven churches in Asia mentioned by John in Revelation?
   Sardis, Thyatira, Philadelphia, Ephesus
4. Who raised Esther as if she was his own daughter?
   Xerxes, Haman, Hegai, Mordecai
5. Who was not involved in writing the book of 2 Thessalonians?
   Paul, Silvanus (Silas), Barnabas, Timotheus (Timothy)
6. Who was the mother of David?
   Not mentioned by name, Sarai, Rebecca, Leah

ANSWERS:

1. New (Eighteenth book of the New Testament)
2. Righteousness (2 Timothy 3:16)
3. Thyatira (Revelation 1:11)
4. Mordecai (Esther 2:7)
5. Barnabas (2 Thessalonians 1:1)
6. Not mentioned by name (Jewish legend says Nitzevet)

Score Correct: _____ Date: _____ Name: _____
Study Notes: _____

_____

_____

Quiz 154

1. Is the book of Zephaniah in the Old Testament, New Testament, or neither?
2. From Proverbs, "Better it is to be of an _____ spirit with the lowly, than to divide the spoil with the proud."
   Genuine, Humble, Adorable, Admirable
3. Who prepared a feast for two (angels) in Sodom, baked unleavened bread, and they did eat?
   Lot, Abel, Ishmael, Hagar
4. What was the more commonly known name of Hadassah?
   Ruth, Esther, Sarah, Michal
5. Which of these describes Amos the prophet in scripture?
   Priest, Herdman, Carpenter, Fisherman
6. What caused the death of Samson's Philistine wife?
   Poisoned, Fell off cliff, Pushed from tower, Burnt with fire

ANSWERS:

1. Old (Thirty-sixth book of the Old Testament)
2. Humble (Proverbs 16:19)
3. Lot (Genesis 19:1–3)
4. Esther (Esther 2:7)
5. Herdman (Amos 7:14)
6. Burnt with fire (Judges 15:4–6)

Score Correct: _____ Date: _____ Name: _____
Study Notes: _____
_____
_____

Quiz 155

1. Is the book of Gabriel in the Old Testament, New Testament, or neither?
2. How long did the east wind blow, as caused by the Lord, to part the Red Sea?
   Seven minutes, All night, Two hours, All day
3. Not only was Satan a murderer from the beginning, but also the father of . . .?
   Sin, Lies, Evil, Lust
4. Who was the only woman to rule over Judah in biblical times?
   Deborah, Dorcas, Eunice, Athaliah
5. According to Jesus, how long will poor people be around?
   Always, Sometimes, Never, 40 years
6. From Acts 20, how many months did Paul stay in Greece?
   3, 5, 7, 9

ANSWERS:

1. Neither (Archangel who announced to the Virgin Mary she had been chosen to bear the Son of God)
2. All night (Exodus 14:21)
3. Lies (John 8:44)
4. Athaliah (2 Chronicles 22:8–12)
5. Always (Mark 14:7)
6. 3 (Acts 20:1–3)

Score Correct: _____ Date: _____ Name: _____
Study Notes: _____
_____
_____

Quiz 156

1. Is the book of Habakkuk in the Old Testament, New Testament, or neither?
2. Jesus said, "This cup is the _____ _____ in my blood: this do ye, as oft as ye drink it, in remembrance of me."
   Given law, New testament, Broken body, Everlasting life
3. After he fled Egypt, whose flock did Moses keep and lead to the back side of the desert?
   Eleazar, Eli, Zadok, Jethro
4. Upon which mountain did Deborah defeat the forces of Sisera?
   Tabor, Zeus, Sinai, Olives
5. Where did the Apostle Paul send Tychicus?
   Rome, Alexandria, Ephesus, Antioch
6. Who was the mate of Sapphira?
   Moses, Ananias, Potiphar, Zimri

ANSWERS:

1. Old (Thirty-fifth book of the Old Testament)
2. New testament (1 Corinthians 11:25)
3. Jethro (His father-in-law) (Exodus 3:1)
4. Tabor (Judges 4:6, 12, 14)
5. Ephesus (2 Timothy 4:12)
6. Ananias (Acts 5:1)

Score Correct: _____ Date: _____ Name: _____
Study Notes: _____
_____
_____

Quiz 157

1. Is the book of Acacia in the Old Testament, New Testament, or neither?
2. From John 21, how many times did Jesus ask Peter, "Lovest thou me"?
   2, 3, 4, 5
3. Who was bespoken by an angel to save Israel from the Midianites?
   Ishmael, Job, Gideon, Philip
4. From Exodus 9, who made a false confession to Aaron and Moses?
   Herod, Malachi, Satan, Pharaoh
5. Who's the only Egyptian queen mentioned in the Bible?
   Sarah, Tahpenes, Ruth, Tamar
6. The Levitical town of Mishal or Mashal was in the territory of?
   Bashan, Asher, Philistia, Corinthia

ANSWERS:
1. Neither (Tree available during biblical times known for density and strength)
2. 3 (John 21:17)
3. Gideon (Judges 6:11–14)
4. Pharaoh (Exodus 9:27)
5. Tahpenes (1 Kings 11:18–19)
6. Asher (Joshua 21:30, 1 Chronicles 6:74)

Score Correct: _____ Date: _____ Name: _____
Study Notes: _____
_____
_____

Quiz 158

1. Is the book of Patara in the Old Testament, New Testament, or neither?
2. While speaking to the church elders, who commented, "And when the chief Shepherd shall appear, ye shall receive a crown of glory that fadeth not away"?
   Peter, Mark, Luke, Thomas
3. From Leviticus 19, the fruit of a newly planted tree must not be eaten until which year?
   2nd, 3rd, 4th, 5th
4. What was Bathsheba doing on the roof when David first saw her?
   Bathing, Praying, Singing, Hiding
5. Which minor prophet predicted a famine of "hearing the words of the Lord"?
   Haggai, Zechariah, Amos, Malachi.
6. What notoriously wicked woman married King Ahab?
   Candace, Shiprah, Adah, Jezebel

ANSWERS:

1. Neither (City on the SW coast of Lycia, today's southern Turkey)
2. Peter (1 Peter 5:1–4)
3. 5th (Leviticus 19:23–25)
4. Bathing (2 Samuel 11:2–3)
5. Amos (Amos 8:11)
6. Jezebel (1 Kings 21:25)

Score Correct: _____ Date: _____ Name: _____
Study Notes: _____
_____
_____

Quiz 159

1. Is the book of Rufus in the Old Testament, New Testament, or neither?
2. Who commanded the rebel army when Absalom rebelled against David?
   Arioch, Abner, Abishai, Amasa
3. In Proverbs, "Surely the churning of milk bringeth forth _____."
   Cheese, Abundance, Strife, Butter
4. Who, or what, cannot be tempted with evil?
   God, Righteous soul, Antichrist, Prophet
5. Job suffered from what physical affliction?
   Deafness, Boils, Blindness, Coughs
6. What's the Sea of Galilee called in John 6?
   Tiberias, Dead, Jordan, Geneva

ANSWERS:
1. Neither (Son of Simon the Cyrenian)
2. Amasa (2 Samuel 17:24–25)
3. Butter (Proverbs 30:33)
4. God (James 1:13)
5. Boils (Job 2:7)
6. Tiberias (John 6:1)

Score Correct: _____ Date: _____ Name: _____
Study Notes: _____
_____
_____

Quiz 160

1. Is the book of Jaffa in the Old Testament, New Testament, or neither?
2. Which of these descriptive articles of clothing or coverings are mentioned in thirty-six verses, while all others have no listing in scripture?
   Robe(s), Cloak(s), Shawl(s), Turban(s)
3. Solomon says that feeding a hungry enemy and giving a thirsty enemy a drink will be like doing "what" upon his head?
   Pounding temple, Heaping burning coals, Covering with shawl, Washing with soap
4. Of the three women Samson was involved with, which was the only one that he married by name or description?
   Woman from Timnah, Deliah, Harlot from Gaza, Judith
5. "Behold, the fear of the Lord, that is wisdom; and to depart from evil is _____."
   Freedom, Understanding, Everlasting, Smartness
6. How many books of the Bible begin with the letter "R"?
   1, 2, 3, 4

ANSWERS:

1. Neither (Ancient Levantine port city founded by the Canaanites)
2. Robe(s) (thirty-six listings, including four in Revelation)
3. Heaping burning coals (Proverbs 25:21–22)
4. Woman from Timnah (Judges 14:1–2)
5. Understanding (Job 28:28)
6. 3 (Revelation, Romans, Ruth)

Score Correct: _____ Date: _____ Name: _____
Study Notes: _____
_____
_____

Samson destroys the gates of Gaza
Courtesy of: clipart.christiansunite.com

Quiz 161

1. Is the book of Ruth in the Old Testament, New Testament, or neither?
2. How many placed their faith in Christ because of Peter's lifting up his voice to the Jews on Pentecost?
   1000, 2000, 3000, 4000
3. To whom did God say, "Before I formed thee in the belly I knew thee; and ordained thee a prophet unto the nations"?
   Daniel, Jeremiah, Noah, Thomas
4. Only once is the phrase, "holier than thou," found in scripture; in what book is it found?
   1 Kings, Ezra, Amos, Isaiah
5. From Genesis 21 who was commander of Abimelech's army?
   Benaiah, Omri, Sisera, Phichol
6. Who was called the light of Israel?
   Ishbibenob, Jesus, Mephibosheth, David

ANSWERS:

1. Old (Eighth book of the Old Testament, and one of two books named after a woman)
2. 3000 (Acts 2:1, 38–41)
3. Jeremiah (Jeremiah 1:5)
4. Isaiah (Isaiah 65:5)
5. Phichol (Genesis 21:22)
6. David (2 Samuel 21:16–17)

Score Correct: _____ Date: _____ Name: _____
Study Notes: _____
_____
_____

Quiz 162

1. Is the book of Gad in the Old Testament, New Testament, or neither?
2. Whom did Jesus address when He said, "The spirit indeed is willing, but the flesh is weak"?
   Mark, Luke, John, Peter
3. In what book is the phrase, "the nations are as a drop of a bucket" (as compared to God's greatness)?
   Exodus, Isaiah, Habakkuk, Malachi
4. From Proverbs, what kind of son maketh a glad father, while a foolish man despiseth his mother?
   Loving, Mindful, Loyal, Wise
5. In Revelation 21's vision, what will not exist in the world to come?
   Sky, Mountain, Sea, Darkness
6. What's the only animal/creature in the Bible that tells a lie?
   Serpent, Camel, Donkey, Dove

ANSWERS:

1. Neither (One of the twelve sons of Jacob)
2. Peter (Matthew 26:40–41)
3. Isaiah (Isaiah 40:14–15)
4. Wise (Proverbs 15:20)
5. Sea (Revelation 21:1)
6. Serpent (Genesis 3:4, 13)

Score Correct: _____ Date: _____ Name: _____
Study Notes: _____
_____
_____

Quiz 163

1. Is the book of Armoni in the Old Testament, New Testament, or neither?
2. From Romans, "For there is no difference between the Jew and the Greek: for the same Lord over all is _____ unto all that call upon him."
   There, Rich, Understanding, Receiving
3. In Psalms, it asserts that one day in the courts of the Lord is better than how many elsewhere in wickedness?
   Ten, Hundred, Thousand, Five thousand
4. How many strong men of Jericho wanted to go and look for Elijah for Elisha?
   Two, Ten, Twenty, Fifty
5. What did a fearful Peter utter when he prayed scripture's shortest prayer?
   Lord save me, Forgive them Father, Please help me, Give me strength
6. And Solomon slept with his fathers, and was buried in the city of?
   Arbah, Shechem, Nahor, David

ANSWERS:

1. Neither (One of Saul's two sons by his concubine Rizpah)
2. Rich (Romans 10:12)
3. Thousand (Psalms 84:9–10)
4. Fifty (2 Kings 2:15–16)
5. Lord save me (Matthew 14:29–31)
6. David (2 Chronicles 9:30–31)

Score Correct: _____ Date: _____ Name: _____
Study Notes: _____
_____
_____

Quiz 164

1. Is the book of Andrew in the Old Testament, New Testament, or neither?
2. Who was David's eldest brother whose anger was kindled when David's pride and naughtiness brought him to the battle lines?
   Abner, Omri, Amasa, Eliab
3. Who was not one of Saul's sons killed in battle by the Philistines?
   Jonathan, Abinadab, Abishai, Malchishua
4. Jesus said in Matthew 22:14, "For many are called, but few are _____."
   Worthy, Chosen, Winners, Liked
5. In Proverbs, what does a merry heart maketh, a cheerful . . . ?
   Countenance, Servant, Giver, Shepherd
6. Jesus saw Satan fall out of heaven as?
   Lightning, Wolf, Serpent, Cat

ANSWERS:
1. Neither (One of the apostles and brother of Simon Peter)
2. Eliab (1 Samuel 17:26–28)
3. Abishai (1 Samuel 31:2)
4. Chosen (Matthew 22:14)
5. Countenance (Proverbs 15:13)
6. Lightning (Luke 10:18)

Score Correct: _____ Date: _____ Name: _____
Study Notes: _____
_____
_____

Quiz 165

1. Is the book of Bochim in the Old Testament, New Testament, or neither?
2. Fill in the blank with the same word: "Now the Lord of _____ himself give you _____ always by all means."
   Love, Peace, Light, Grace
3. The book of Lamentations mourns the conquest of Jerusalem and compares the once great city to a . . . ?
   Desert, Beggar, Prisoner, Widow
4. Lotan, Shobal, Zibeon, and Anah were among the sons of what Horite father?
   Beor, Seir, Husham, Jobab
5. In Luke 3, who told Roman soldiers to avoid taking money by force?
   John the Baptist, Paul, Mark, Matthew
6. Which natural disaster occurred only once in a great way in the Bible?
   Windstorm, Flood, Drought, Earthquake

ANSWERS:

1. Neither (Place situated west of the River Jordan)
2. Peace (2 Thessalonians 3:16)
3. Widow (Lamentations 1:1)
4. Seir (Genesis 36:20)
5. John the Baptist (Luke 3:12–16)
6. Flood (Genesis 8:13, 21)

Score Correct: _____ Date: _____ Name: _____
Study Notes: _____
_____
_____

Quiz 166

1. Is the book of Barad in the Old Testament, New Testament, or neither?
2. Under siege by the Assyrians, what king constructed a conduit (tunnel) that would ensure Jerusalem's water supply?
   Menshem, Jeroboam, Ahaz, Hezekiah
3. When a voice came out of the cloud at Jesus's transfiguration, what did it say regarding, "This is my beloved Son"?
   Love him, Hear him, Obey him, Honor him
4. Who was described as "from his shoulders and upward he was higher than any of the people"?
   Goliath, Saul, Jesse, Kish
5. According to the first verse in Psalms 96 and 98, what should we sing to the Lord?
   New song, Old memory, Joyful noise, Glad tidings
6. In Romans 1, Paul said, "For I am not ashamed of the _____ of Christ."
   Word, Love, Redemption, Gospel

ANSWERS:

1. Neither (Hebrew name of one of the plagues that God cast on Egypt)
2. Hezekiah (2 Kings 20:20)
3. Hear him (Mark 9:2, 7)
4. Saul (1 Samuel 9:2)
5. New song (Psalms 96:1, Psalms 98:1)
6. Gospel (Romans 1:1, 16)

Score Correct: _____ Date: _____ Name: _____
Study Notes: _____
_____
_____

Quiz 167

1. Is the book of Thaddaeus in the Old Testament, New Testament, or neither?
2. Who, along with all his coconspirators, was swallowed up by the earth after objecting to Moses's authority?
   Korah, Kelub, Keran, Kileab
3. With well doing you may silence the ignorance of what "type" of men?
   Young, Warrior, Abiding, Foolish
4. Which of these phrases did Pilate ask Jesus?
   Where is God?, Why are you here?, What is truth?, How old are you?
5. Who contracted leprosy for lying and disobedience to the prophet Elisha?
   Deborah, Gideon, Gehazi, Matthew
6. What are the names of Abaddon and Apollyon used to denote?
   Satan, Constellations, Mountains, Idols

ANSWERS:

1. Neither (One of the twelve original apostles)
2. Korah (Numbers 16:1–2, 20–21, 31–33)
3. Foolish (1 Peter 2:15)
4. What is truth? (John 18:37–38)
5. Gehazi (2 Kings 5:21, 25–27)
6. Satan (Revelation 9:11)

Score Correct: _____ Date: _____ Name: _____

Study Notes: _____

_____

_____

Quiz 168

1. Is the book of Sadducees in the Old Testament, New Testament, or neither?
2. To keep Paul humble, God gave Paul a thorn in the flesh. Paul pleaded how many times for it to be taken away?
   2, 3, 4, 5
3. How should Christians act toward ones that have the rule over them (referring to elders)?
   Respectfully, In submission, Cheerfully, Timidly
4. What happens to those who judge others?
   Condemn themselves, Are fools, Become hypocrites, Lose faith
5. Shamgar, the son of Anath, slew six hundred Philistine men with an ox . . . ?
   Jawbone, Yoke, Goad, Horn
6. Who was the Roman governor of Syris at the time of Jesus's birth?
   Archelaus, Cyrenius, Felix, Cumanus

ANSWERS:

1. Neither (Group of wealthy Jewish leaders during Jesus's lifetime)
2. 3 (2 Corinthians 12:7–8)
3. In submission (Hebrews 13:17)
4. Condemn themselves (Romans 2:1)
5. Goad (Prodding rod) (Judges 3:31, 5:6)
6. Cyrenius (Luke 2:1–2)

Score Correct: _____ Date: _____ Name: _____
Study Notes: _____
_____
_____

Quiz 169

1. Is the book of Matthew in the Old Testament, New Testament, or neither?
2. In Proverbs, "He that hath no rule over his own spirit is like a city that is broken down, and _____ _____."
   With sin, Going away, Without walls, Evils abound
3. From Exodus 1, what were the people of Israel forced to make by the Egyptians?
   Blankets, Boats, Baskets, Bricks
4. What person's last recorded words in scripture were, "My Lord and my God"?
   Samson, Matthew, Thomas, David
5. The men of Athens had an altar with an inscription to the . . . ?
   Golden calf, Unknown God, Silver spoon, Sun god
6. Who was the meekest (most humble) man on earth?
   Jacob, Elijah, Noah, Moses

ANSWERS:

1. New (First book of the New Testament)
2. Without walls (Proverbs 25:28)
3. Bricks (and mortar) (Exodus 1:13–14)
4. Thomas (John 20:27–28)
5. Unknown God (Acts 17:22–23)
6. Moses (Numbers 12:2–3)

Score Correct: _____ Date: _____ Name: _____
Study Notes: _____
_____
_____

Quiz 170

1. Is the book of Sardis in the Old Testament, New Testament, or neither?
2. What Athenian Areopagite (court judge) was converted under Paul's preaching?
   Dionysius, Hemdan, Anan, Olympas
3. From Exodus 20, to whom did God give the Ten Commandments?
   Noah, Abraham, Moses, Aaron
4. What Hebrew became second-in-command (prime minister) to Pharaoh?
   David, Joseph, Nehemiah, Joel
5. How many times does the word "grandmother" occur in scripture?
   0, 1, 3, 6
6. Where was Jesus brought up, as mentioned in Luke 4?
   Smyrna, Tarsus, Antioch, Nazareth

ANSWERS:

1. Neither (Ancient city, capital of the Lydian Empire, and one of Seven Churches of Revelation)
2. Dionysius (Acts 17:21, 34)
3. Moses (Exodus 19:25, 20:1–2)
4. Joseph (Genesis 41:41–42)
5. 1 (2 Timothy 1:5)
6. Nazareth (Luke 4:14–16)

Score Correct: _____ Date: _____ Name: _____
Study Notes: _____
_____
_____

Quiz 171

1. Is the book of Haggith in the Old Testament, New Testament, or neither?
2. What is the shortest book in the Old Testament by counting the number of words in Hebrew or Greek?
   Job, Joel, Obadiah, Zechariah
3. Who was stoned to death in the valley of Achor, along with his children and livestock?
   Abinoam, Achan, Ahilud, Abitub
4. What kind of "duty" of man is to "Fear God, and keep his commandments"?
   Sworn, Whole, Solemn, Promised
5. Who did Jacob kiss, after which he lifted up his voice and wept?
   Rachel, Leah, Sarai, Rebekah
6. What man, although warned, invited his slayer(s) to a feast?
   Nebat, Gedaliah, Shelah, Asaiah

ANSWERS:

1. Neither (A wife of David and mother of Adonijah)
2. Obadiah (440 words)
3. Achan (Joshua 7:24–25)
4. Whole (Ecclesiastes 12:13)
5. Rachel (Genesis 29:11)
6. Gedaliah (Jeremiah 40:15–16, 41:1–2)

Score Correct: _____ Date: _____ Name: _____
Study Notes: _____
_____
_____

Quiz 172

1. Is the book of Cherubim in the Old Testament, New Testament, or neither?
2. Moses was eighty while Aaron was how old when they spoke to Pharaoh about letting their people go?
   60, 74, 83, 90
3. Which two books of the Bible contain the Ten Commandments?
   Genesis, Exodus, Leviticus, Deuteronomy, Joshua
4. What were the first words God spoke to humankind?
   Worship the Lord, Be fruitful, Love thy neighbor, You breathe
5. From Luke 8, how many demons did Mary Magdalene have in her?
   1, 3, 5, 7
6. Who is/was father to the fatherless and a judge of the widows?
   Solomon, Heaven, Geber, God

ANSWERS:

1. Neither (Winged creatures supportive of God)
2. 83 (Exodus 7:7)
3. Exodus, Deuteronomy (Exodus 20:2–17, Deuteronomy 5:6–21)
4. Be fruitful (Genesis 1:28)
5. 7 (Luke 8:2)
6. God (Psalms 68:5)

Score Correct: _____ Date: _____ Name: _____
Study Notes: _____
_____
_____

Quiz 173

1. Is the book of Eli in the Old Testament, New Testament, or neither?
2. From Ephesians, according to the prince the power of the air now worketh in the children of . . . ?
   Wrath, Disobedience, Spite, Hunger
3. When Jeroboam went out of Jerusalem, what Shilonite did he meet dressed in a new garment?
   Shelah, Ahijah, Judah, Jehoahaz
4. How many years did Tola, the son of Puah and grandson of Dodo, judge Israel?
   1, 7, 23, 110
5. Who erected a pillar (memorial) to himself because he did not have a son?
   Onesimus, Absalom, Spartacus, Isaiah
6. From Genesis 37, who had a coat of many colours?
   Abraham, Goliath, Adam, Joseph

ANSWERS:

1. Neither (High priest who served forty years as judge of Israel)
2. Disobedience (Ephesians 2:2)
3. Ahijah (1 Kings 11:29)
4. 23 (Judges 10:1–2)
5. Absalom (2 Samuel 18:18)
6. Joseph (Genesis 37:3)

Score Correct: _____ Date: _____ Name: _____
Study Notes: _____
_____
_____

Quiz 174

1. Is the book of James in the Old Testament, New Testament, or neither?
2. Who had a rod that God turned into a serpent that swallowed up the Pharaoh's sorcerers' rods that also had been turned into serpents?
   Noah, Aaron, Abraham, Isaac
3. Which of the mighty men of David fought so long that his weary hand stuck to the hilt of his sword?
   Ishbaal, Eleazar, Dodo, Shammah
4. Who tells Naaman that he should travel to the prophet Elisha and ask for healing from his leprosy?
   Little maid, Young boy, Old beggar, Seductive mistress
5. Jesus said, "If thou canst believe, all things are _____ to him that believeth."
   Forthcoming, Possible, Granted, Coming
6. What is the first city mentioned in scripture?
   Machaerus, Tel Megiddo, Qumran, Enoch

ANSWERS:
1. New (Twentieth book of the New Testament)
2. Aaron (Exodus 7:9–12)
3. Eleazar (2 Samuel 23:9–10)
4. Little maid (2 Kings 5:1–3, 9–10)
5. Possible (Mark 9:23)
6. Enoch (Genesis 4:17)

Score Correct: _____ Date: _____ Name: _____
Study Notes: _____
_____
_____

Quiz 175

1. Is the book of Hagarites in the Old Testament, New Testament, or neither?
2. Fill in the blanks with the same word: "For thou shalt worship no other god: for the Lord, whose name is _____, is a _____ God."
   Righteous, Jealous, Devine, Jehovah
3. For how long was the Ark of the Lord in the country of the Philistines and away from the Israelites?
   40 days and nights, 3 months, 7 months, 12 years
4. After dying from her childbirth of Benjamin, Rachel was buried on the way to . . . ?
   Assyria, Ephrath, Shur, Havilah
5. With who did the apostle Paul leave his cloak at Troas?
   Carpus, Abijam, Dodo, Hezir
6. What was the previous name of Hebron?
   Luz, Jubus, Kirjatharba, Hazazon-tamar

ANSWERS:

1. Neither (A people dwelling in Gilead to the east of Palestine)
2. Jealous (Exodus 34:14)
3. 7 months (1 Samuel 6:1)
4. Ephrath (Genesis 35:18–19)
5. Carpus (2 Timothy 4:13)
6. Kirjatharba (Joshua 14:15), also Arbah (Genesis 35:27)

Score Correct: _____ Date: _____ Name: _____
Study Notes: _____
_____
_____

Quiz 176

1. Is the book of Miktam in the Old Testament, New Testament, or neither?
2. Fill in the blank from Paul in Romans 8: "There is therefore now no _____ to them which are in Christ Jesus."
   Scorn, Condemnation, Sorrow, Laughter
3. How many times are the words "tomb" or "tombs" specifically mentioned in scripture?
   2, 9, 30, 40
4. How old was David when he began his reign of forty years?
   12, 23, 30, 45
5. Who was married to Joanna and a steward of Herod Antipas?
   Asarelah, Chuza, Kedorlaomer, Likhi
6. What does the helmet represent in the "armor of God"?
   Salvation, Truth, Righteousness, The word

ANSWERS:

1. Neither (A valued object engraved of gold)
2. Condemnation (Romans 8:1)
3. 9 (Job 21:32, Matthew 8:28, 23:29, 27:60, Mark 5:2–3, 5, 6:29, Luke 8:27)
4. 30 (2 Samuel 5:4)
5. Chuza (Luke 8:3)
6. Salvation (Ephesians 6:13, 17)

Score Correct: _____ Date: _____ Name: _____
Study Notes: _____

_____
_____

Quiz 177

1. Is the book of Cain in the Old Testament, New Testament, or neither?
2. Meah, Jezreel, Hananeel, and David are all mentioned as "what" in scripture?
   Rivers, Mountains, Temples, Towers
3. How many lords (kings) did the Philistines have during Samuel's early life?
   One, Two, Five, Ten
4. Who did King Jehosophat appoint as the officer for all the king's matters?
   Meraiah, Zebadiah, Pekahiah, Phlegon
5. What priest was king of the city of Salem and "King of peace"?
   Ezekiel, Seraiah, Melchisedec, Haggai
6. In John 15, Jesus said, "I am the vine, ye are the _____."
   Garden, Branches, Water, Fruit

ANSWERS:

1. Neither (First son of Adam and Eve)
2. Towers: Meah (Nehemiah 12:39), Jezreel (2 Kings 9:17), Hananeel (Jeremiah 31:38), David (Song of Solomon 4:4)
3. Five (Judges 3:3, 1 Samuel 6:4)
4. Zebadiah (2 Chronicles 19:8, 11)
5. Melchisedec (Hebrews 7:1–2)
6. Branches (John 15:5)

Score Correct: _____ Date: _____ Name: _____
Study Notes: _____
_____
_____

Quiz 178

1. Is the book of Bartholomew in the Old Testament, New Testament, or neither?
2. From Proverbs, "He that handleth a matter _____ shall find good: and whoso trusteth in the Lord, happy is he."
   Slowly, Wisely, Surely, Cheerfully
3. What were the people of Judah burning at Topheth in the valley of the son of Hinnom that displeased God?
   Books, Their children, Livestock, Sandals
4. Which punishment was given to a man gathering up sticks in the wilderness on the Sabbath?
   Banishment from camp, Stoned to death, Secluded across river, Seven lashings
5. How long was the rule of Zimri, king of Israel, before the people made Omri the new king?
   7 days, 6 months, 2 years, 5 years
6. Who, or what, is the end of the law for righteousness to everyone that believeth?
   The Bible, Christ, The Word, Faith

ANSWERS:
1. Neither (Apostle of Jesus)
2. Wisely (Proverbs 16:20)
3. Their children (Jeremiah 7:30–33)
4. Stoned to death (Numbers 15:32–36)
5. 7 days (1 Kings 16:15)
6. Christ (Romans 10:4)

Score Correct: _____ Date: _____ Name: _____
Study Notes: _____

_____

_____

Quiz 179

1. Is the book of Numbers in the Old Testament, New Testament, or neither?
2. What did Jesus say about the one who would betray Him while the disciples were eating the Passover meal?
    Loved money, Would not drink, Dippeth his hand with me in the dish, Spilled the wine chalice
3. While on the cross, Christ was offered wine mingled with "what," which He refused?
    Salt, Water, Myrrh, Speck
4. How many years did David reign over Israel?
    7, 33, 40, 57
5. Who was the father of Esau and Jacob?
    Solomon, Isaac, Abraham, Noah
6. What relationship were Moses and Aaron?
    Father/son, Uncle/nephew, Grandfather/grandson, Brothers

ANSWERS:

1. Old (Fourth book of the Old Testament)
2. Dippeth his hand with me in the dish (Matthew 26:20–23)
3. Myrrh (Mark 15:23)
4. 40 (1 Chronicles 29:26–27)
5. Isaac (Genesis 25:21–26)
6. Brothers (Exodus 4:14)

Score Correct: _____ Date: _____ Name: _____
Study Notes: _____
_____
_____

Quiz 180

1. Is the book of 2 Thessalonians in the Old Testament, New Testament, or neither?
2. Who's in command of the largest recorded army in the Bible at two hundred thousand thousand (200 million)?
   4 evil angels, Asa, Gabriel, Jeroboam
3. During which story did God turn Moses's staff into a serpent and back again?
   Parting of Red Sea, Burning bush, Water into wine, David and Goliath
4. Song of Solomon and which other book specifically mention the "apple tree"?
   Genesis, Ezra, Joel, Nahum
5. Besides Israel, what country is to be scattered to every people?
   Joktan, Tiras, Cush, Elam
6. Who was servant Eliakim the son of?
   Shebna, Hilkiah, Joah, Rabshakeh

ANSWERS:

1. New (Fourteen book of the New Testament)
2. 4 evil angels (Revelation 9:15–16)
3. Burning bush (Exodus 3:1–2, 4:2–3)
4. Joel (Song of Solomon 2:3, 8:5, Joel 1:12)
5. Elam (Jeremiah 49:34–36)
6. Hilkiah (Isaiah 22:20)

Score Correct: _____ Date: _____ Name: _____
Study Notes: _____
_____
_____

God appears to Moses in the burning bush
Courtesy of: clipart.christiansunite.com

Quiz 181

1. Is the book of Jude in the Old Testament, New Testament, or neither?
2. In scripture, which Old Testament prophet mentions the Lord's "Book of Remembrance"?
   Huldah, Moses, Iddo, Malachi
3. Eve's name is mentioned only four times in scripture with how many of those four in the book of Genesis?
   1, 2, 3, All 4
4. From Exodus 15, who sang and led a triumphant song after the crossing of the Red Sea?
   Zipporah, Delilah, Miriam, Dinah
5. What chapter of Psalms has four verses that are exactly alike?
   4, 58, 107, 133
6. Who was the second son of Moses and Zipporah?
   Eber, Ebiasaph, Ebronah, Eliezer

ANSWERS:

1. New (Twenty-sixth book of the New Testament)
2. Malachi (Malachi 3:16)
3. 2 (Genesis 3:20, 4:1, 2 Corinthians 11:3, 1 Timothy 2:13).
4. Miriam (Exodus 15:20–21)
5. 107 (Psalms 107:8, 15, 21, 31)
6. Eliezer (Exodus 18:2–4) (Gershom was the first)

Score Correct: _____ Date: _____ Name: _____
Study Notes: _____
_____
_____

Quiz 182

1. Is the book of 4 John in the Old Testament, New Testament, or neither?
2. In the Old Testament, who said, "Speak, Lord; for thy servant heareth"?
   Noah, Isaiah, Samuel, Adam
3. In the book of Joshua, the city of Dan was first called . . . ?
   Leshem, Jebusi, Bela, Ophrah
4. From Esther 5, who was the wife of Haman of Persia?
   Naaman, Zeresh, Not named, Delilah
5. Who was Adam and Eve's youngest son?
   Ishmael, Cain, Abel, Seth
6. Which book follows 2 Chronicles?
   Proverbs, Jeremiah, Isaiah, Ezra

ANSWERS:

1. Neither (Only 1 John, 2 John, 3 John)
2. Samuel (1 Samuel 3:9–10)
3. Leshem (Joshua 19:47)
4. Zeresh (Esther 5:10)
5. Seth (Genesis 4:25)
6. Ezra (Fifteenth book of the Old Testament)

Score Correct: _____ Date: _____ Name: _____
Study Notes: _____
_____
_____

Quiz 183

1. Is the book of Harbona in the Old Testament, New Testament, or neither?
2. From Judges 1, for which Canaanite city did spies from the house of Joseph find the entrance?
    Ai, Sardis, Colossae, Bethel
3. John the Baptist had his raiment (clothes) from the hair of what animal?
    Wolf, Camel, Lion, Goat
4. In Acts 12, what ungodly ruler was struck down by an angel of the Lord?
    Herod, Ehud, Jehu, Abner
5. How many books of the Bible begin with the letter "D"?
    1, 2, 3, 4
6. From Proverbs, "The words of a talebearer are as _____"?
    Truths, Wounds, Answers, Serpents

ANSWERS:

1. Neither (One of the chamberlains of King Ahasuerus)
2. Bethel (Judges 1:23–25)
3. Camel (Matthew 3:1, 4)
4. Herod (Acts 12:21–23)
5. 2 (Deuteronomy, Daniel)
6. Wounds (Proverbs 18:8)

Score Correct: _____ Date: _____ Name: _____
Study Notes: _____
_____
_____

Quiz 184

1. Is the book of Judges in the Old Testament, New Testament, or neither?
2. Whose last words in scripture were, "O God, that I may be at once avenged of the Philistines for my two eyes"?
   Zimri, Paul, Eli, Samson
3. Who assumed if Isaac died that God would be able to bring him back to life?
   Rebekah, Esau, Abraham, Jacob
4. Where was a woman named Damaris converted under Paul's preaching?
   Galatia, Athens, Derbe, Miletus
5. Which two asked to sit at Jesus's right and left hand in heaven?
   James, Thomas, Peter, John
6. Who was the famed brother of Lahmi?
   John the Baptist, Herod, Goliath, Paul

ANSWERS:
1. Old (Seventh book of the Old Testament)
2. Samson (Judges 16:28)
3. Abraham (Hebrews 11:17–19)
4. Athens (Acts 17:21–22, 34)
5. James, John (Mark 10:35–37)
6. Goliath (1 Chronicles 20:5)

Score Correct: _____ Date: _____ Name: _____
Study Notes: _____
_____
_____

Quiz 185

1. Is the book of 1 Peter in the Old Testament, New Testament, or neither?
2. In Mark 7, who said to a Greek woman, "It is not meet [right] to take the children's bread and cast it unto the dogs"?
    Jesus, Judas, Joshua, Jacob
3. Who was the husband of an unnamed prophetess and the father of Shearjashub and Mahershalalhashbaz?
    Isaac, Isaiah, Abraham, Methuselah
4. From Revelation 8, when the third angel sounded, what was the falling star called?
    Armageddon, Wormwood, Rapture, Zabulon
5. Concerning Paul, who/what was "Crescens," as implied?
    Faithful dog, His staff, Coworker, His tentmaker
6. Who proclaimed a fast at the river of Ahava?
    David, Adonikam, Ezra, Ariel

ANSWERS:

1. New (Twenty-first book of the New Testament)
2. Jesus (Mark 7:25–27)
3. Isaiah (Isaiah 7:3, 8:3)
4. Wormwood (Revelation 8:10–11)
5. Coworker (2 Timothy 4:10)
6. Ezra (Ezra 8:15, 21)

Score Correct: _____ Date: _____ Name: _____
Study Notes: _____

_____

_____

Quiz 186

1. Is the book of 3 Chronicles in the Old Testament, New Testament, or neither?
2. What prophet confronted King Ahab about forsaking the commandments of the Lord and the idolatry of the people?
   Silas, Elijah, Iddo, Phinehas
3. Who were some philosophers in Athens referring to when they asked, "What will this babbler say"?
   Menander, Paul, Epimenides, Aratus
4. From 2 Chronicles, who passed all the kings of the earth in riches and wisdom?
   Asa, Solomon, Jehoshaphat, Jehoram
5. Whose sons were Nadab the firstborn, and Abihu, Eleazar, and Ithamar?
   Joshua, Aaron, Moses, Mordecai
6. The devil tempted Jesus to turn what inanimate objects into bread?
   Wood chips, Stones, Twigs, Leaves

ANSWERS:
1. Neither (Only 1 Chronicles, 2 Chronicles)
2. Elijah (1 Kings 18:17–19)
3. Paul (Acts 17:16–18)
4. Solomon (2 Chronicles 9:22–23)
5. Aaron (Numbers 3:2)
6. Stones (Matthew 4:1–3)

Score Correct: _____ Date: _____ Name: _____
Study Notes: _____
_____
_____

Quiz 187

1. Is the book of Deuteronomy in the Old Testament, New Testament, or neither?
2. Who did the Lord express to in the night by a vision, "Be not afraid, but speak, and hold not thy peace"?
   Daniel, Paul, Peter, Joseph
3. What was like coriander seed, white, and the taste of it was like wafers made with honey?
   Leek dip, Manna, Bread at Last Supper, Fava beans
4. From Proverbs, "A word fitly spoken is like _____ of gold in pictures of silver."
   Songs, Talents, Trinkets, Apples
5. In 2 Peter 1, what were holy men moved by in regard to prophecy?
   Kindred spirit, Holy Ghost, Sins, Love of God
6. Who became the twelfth apostle, replacing Judas Iscariot?
   Mordeci, Matthias, Stephen, Timothy

ANSWERS:

1. Old (Fifth book of the Old Testament)
2. Paul (Acts 18:9)
3. Manna (Exodus 16:31)
4. Apples (Proverbs 25:11)
5. Holy Ghost (2 Peter 1:21)
6. Matthias (Acts 1:26)

Score Correct: _____ Date: _____ Name: _____
Study Notes: _____
_____
_____

Quiz 188

1. Is the book of Quartus in the Old Testament, New Testament, or neither?
2. What was the young virgin's name that King David's servants brought to him to keep him warm as he was old and stricken with age?
   Tamar, Abishag, Almah, Parthenos
3. From 1 Chronicles, who said, "For all things come of thee, and of thine own have we given thee"?
   Jacob, David, Paul, Job
4. In scripture, who was known as the "supplanter"?
   Aaron, Moses, Jacob, Hosea
5. From the book of Exodus, who took the bones of Joseph with him?
   Noah, Moses, Abraham, Isaac
6. Which of these women appeared the earliest in scripture?
   Miriam, Deborah, Rachel, Naomi

ANSWERS:

1. Neither (Corinthian Christian who joined Paul in sending greetings to friends at Rome)
2. Abishag (1 Kings 1:1–3)
3. David (1 Chronicles 29:10–14)
4. Jacob (Genesis 27:36)
5. Moses (Exodus 13:19)
6. Rachel (Genesis 29)

Score Correct: _____ Date: _____ Name: _____
Study Notes: _____
_____
_____

Quiz 189

1. Is the book of Psalms in the Old Testament, New Testament, or neither?
2. Who hid himself and survived the slaying of threescore and ten persons on one stone by Abimelech and his hired assailants?
    Jotham, Elmadam, Guni, Hezro
3. What did Paul suggest to Timothy for his stomach's sake and his often infirmities?
    Water, Wine, Bread, Honey
4. From Judges 6, what son of Joash threshed wheat by the winepress?
    Gideon, Joash, Neco, Hosea
5. Which was not a biblical nationality in scripture?
    Hittites, Girgashites, Penorites, Jebusites
6. What was the city of Bethel's previous name?
    Luz, Nina, Salem, Kiriath-Arba

ANSWERS:

1. Old (Nineteenth book of the Old Testament)
2. Jotham (Judges 9:1–5)
3. Wine (1 Timothy 5:23)
4. Gideon (Judges 6:11)
5. Penorites (Fictious, Joshua 24:11)
6. Luz (Judges 1:23)

Score Correct: _____ Date: _____ Name: _____
Study Notes: _____
_____
_____

Quiz 190

1. Is the book of Abana in the Old Testament, New Testament, or neither?
2. At the conclusion of his numerous letters, how does Paul tell his readers to greet each other?
   Reverent chant, Holy kiss, Joyous hug, Hearty handshake
3. Who was the daughter of Amminadab and sister of Naashon that married Aaron?
   Jehosheba, Elisheba, Achsah, Puah
4. Job said the fear of the Lord is wisdom; and what is to depart from evil?
   Goodness, Happiness, Victory, Understanding
5. How many books of the Bible begin with the letter "L"?
   1, 2, 3, 4
6. Shechem was the son of . . . ?
   James, Hamor, Jacob, Onan

ANSWERS:

1. Neither (River of Damascus)
2. Holy kiss (1 Thessalonians 5:26, Romans 16:16, 2 Corinthians 13:12)
3. Elisheba (Exodus 6:23)
4. Understanding (Job 28:28)
5. 3 (Lamentations, Leviticus, Luke)
6. Hamor (Genesis 34:2)

Score Correct: _____ Date: _____ Name: _____
Study Notes: _____
_____
_____

Quiz 191

1. Is the book of Smyrna in the Old Testament, New Testament, or neither?
2. From Proverbs, "Whoso boasteth himself of a false gift is like clouds and wind without ____"?
   Meaning, Hope, Breeze, Rain
3. From what type of person did Saul seek relief when an evil spirit tormented him?
   Harpist, Sorceress, Madman, Soldier
4. Jesus said, "Heaven and earth shall pass away, but my _____ shall not."
   Life, Children, Love, Words
5. Which was known as the "city of the priests" because it had so many?
   Bozrah, Nob, Edrei, Chun
6. What daughter of Leah and Jacob was defiled by Shechem?
   Bathsheba, Dinah, Elisabeth, Anna

ANSWERS:

1. Neither (One of Seven Churches of Revelation, aka the Seven Churches of the Apocalypse)
2. Rain (Proverbs 25:14)
3. Harpist (1 Samuel 16:14–16)
4. Words (Matthew 24:35)
5. Nob (1 Samuel 22:19)
6. Dinah (Genesis 34:1–2)

Score Correct: _____ Date: _____ Name: _____
Study Notes: _____
_____
_____

Quiz 192

1. Is the book of Gomer in the Old Testament, New Testament, or neither?
2. What nation defeated the northern kingdom of Israel and relocated its people and brought them unto Halah, Habor, Hara, and to the river Gozan?
   Babylon, Assyria, Egypt, Persia
3. Who answered the Lord about from where he came, "From walking up and down in it (the earth)"?
   Moses, Abraham, Satan, Aaron
4. Which king unwittingly signed a decree causing Daniel to be thrown into the lions' den?
   Menahem, Pekah, Darius, Baasha
5. What "woman of" this place is the only one in scripture described as a wench (maidservant)?
   Enrogel, Gilead, Damascus, Engedi
6. To whom did Jesus say, "I will give unto thee the keys of the kingdom of heaven"?
   Andrew, Peter, Cornelius, Malchus

ANSWERS:

1. Neither (Among its biblical mentions, one as the wife or concubine of Hosea)
2. Assyria (1 Chronicles 5:26)
3. Satan (Job 1:7)
4. Darius (Daniel 6:7–9, 13–15)
5. Enrogel (2 Samuel 17:17)
6. Peter (Matthew 16:18–19)

Score Correct: _____ Date: _____ Name: _____
Study Notes: _____
_____
_____

Quiz 193

1. Is the book of Nahum in the Old Testament, New Testament, or neither?
2. Where in scripture does it say that Satan knows and hears our inner thoughts?
   Nowhere, 2 Peter 2:4, James 4:7, Matthew 10:1
3. What is the number of years that is like one day to the Lord?
   10, 100, 1000, 5000
4. Which group of consecrated men did not cut their hair?
   Canaanites, Midianites, Nazarites, Hagarites
5. In scripture, who/what was Mahanaim?
   Messenger, Mountain, Ford, Place
6. Who was the mother of Moses?
   Abigail, Jochebed, Elisheba, Athaliah

ANSWERS:

1. Old (Thirty-fourth book of the Old Testament)
2. Nowhere (Nothing in scripture indicates Satan is omniscient)
3. 1000 (2 Peter 3:8)
4. Nazarites (Numbers 6:1, 5)
5. Place (On the east of the Jordan) (Genesis 32:2)
6. Jochebed (Exodus 6:20, Numbers 26:59)

Score Correct: _____ Date: _____ Name: _____

Study Notes: _____

_____

_____

Quiz 194

1. Is the book of Etham in the Old Testament, New Testament, or neither?
2. What method of death was for a man who blasphemed the Lord's name with a curse?
   Hanging, Stoning, Starvation, Beaten
3. Who used handkerchiefs and aprons to heal the sick and drive out demons?
   Jesus, Paul, Mark, Jeremiah
4. From John 6, what substance or area did Jesus miraculously walk upon?
   Sea, Fire, Clouds, Broken bones
5. What did God call the firmament?
   Rapture, Armageddon, Passover, Heaven
6. From Romans 6, what are the wages of sin?
   Riches, Eternal life, Death, Freedom

ANSWERS:

1. Neither (One of the Stations of the Exodus)
2. Stoning (Leviticus 24:16)
3. Paul (Acts 19:11–12)
4. Sea (John 6:19)
5. Heaven (Genesis 1:8)
6. Death (Romans 6:23)

Score Correct: _____ Date: _____ Name: _____
Study Notes: _____
_____
_____

Quiz 195: Love Flavored

1. Is the book of Valentine in the Old, New Testament, or neither?
2. From 1 John 3, "Let us not love in word, neither in tongue; but in deed and in . . ."?
   Hope, Abundance, Touch, Truth
3. Which Old Testament book reads like a love story between a bride and groom?
   Ruth, Daniel, Habakkuk, Song of Solomon
4. In Proverbs 10, "Hatred stirreth up strifes: but love covereth all. . ."?
   Sins, Beings, Creation, Enemies
5. Where does one find the phrase, "God is love"?
   Genesis, Nehemiah, Hebrews, 1 John
6. From Hebrews 13, what is honorable in all?
   Love, Trust, Marriage, Worship

ANSWERS:

1. Neither (Romantic name used throughout Europe)
2. Truth (1 John 3:18)
3. Song of Solomon (Passionate poem professing their love)
4. Sins (Proverbs 10:12)
5. 1 John (1 John 4:8, 16)
6. Marriage (Hebrews 13:4)

Score Correct: _____ Date: _____ Name: _____
Study Notes: _____
_____
_____

Quiz 196: Evil Flavored

1. Is the book of Asmodeus in the Old Testament, New Testament, or neither?
2. From Matthew 12, when an evil spirit returns to a person, how many companions does it bring?
   2, 3, 7, 16
3. In which book's chapter 22 is it stated, "Thou shalt not suffer a witch to live"?
   Exodus, Numbers, Isaiah, Hebrews
4. Who called the city of Nineveh the mistress of witchcrafts?
   Ahab, Nahum, Lucifer, Peter
5. What king of Israel was tormented by an evil spirit?
   Solomon, David, Elah, Saul
6. What number is the mark of the beast?
   4, 7, 133, 666

ANSWERS:

1. Neither (A king of demons in the legends of constructing Solomon's Temple)
2. 7 (Matthew 12:43–45)
3. Exodus (Exodus 22:18)
4. Nahum (Nahum 3:4–7)
5. Saul (1 Samuel 16:14–15)
6. 666 (Revelation 13:18)

Score Correct: _____ Date: _____ Name: _____
Study Notes: _____
_____
_____

Quiz 197: Labour Flavored

1. Is the book of Labour in the Old Testament, New Testament, or neither?
2. Fill in the blanks with the same word: "Labour not for the _____ which perisheth, but for that _____ which endureth unto everlasting life."
   Fruit, Meat, Payment, Love
3. In 1 Kings 5, how many thousand men comprised the labour force that King Solomon raised?
   1, 5, 10, 30
4. From which biblical account or passage are ones directed to rest from work?
   Sermon on the Mount, Feeding of the 5000, Ten Commandments, David and Goliath
5. In the book of Deuteronomy, how many days shalt thou labour and do all thy work?
   Two, Four, Six, Seven
6. Proverbs 14 states, "In all labour there is _____"?
   Love, Hope, Light, Profit

ANSWERS:
1. Neither
2. Meat (John 6:27)
3. 30 (1 Kings 5:13)
4. Ten Commandments (Exodus 20:9–10)
5. Six (Deuteronomy 5:13–14)
6. Profit (Proverbs 14:23)

Score Correct: _____ Date: _____ Name: _____
Study Notes: _____
_____
_____

Quiz 198: Liberty Flavored

1. Is the book of Cheirut in the Old Testament, New Testament, or neither?
2. In Galatians, "Only do not use your freedom as an opportunity for the flesh, but through _____ serve one another." Friendship, Honesty, Love, Hope
3. From 2 Corinthians, "Now the Lord is that Spirit: and where the Spirit of the Lord is, there is _____." Hope, Freedom, Love, Liberty
4. In John 8, "If the _____ therefore shall make you free, ye shall be free indeed." Heart, Worship, Celebration, Son
5. From what book's 6:7 does it say, "For he that is dead is freed from sin"? Isaiah, Daniel, Mark, Romans
6. How many times is the word "independence" mentioned in the Bible? 0, 2, 11, 17

ANSWERS:
1. Neither (Hebrew word for freedom)
2. Love (Galatians 5:13)
3. Liberty (2 Corinthians 3:17)
4. Son (John 8:36)
5. Romans (Romans 6:7)
6. 0 (No mention in the Bible)

Score Correct: _____ Date: _____ Name: _____
Study Notes: _____
_____
_____

Quiz 199: Thanksgiving Flavored

1. Is the book of Shukria in the Old Testament, New Testament, or neither?
2. In 2 Timothy, what kinds of people does Paul list as being signs of the last days?
   Adulterers, Sun worshippers, Renegades, Unthankful people
3. From Psalms, "O give thanks unto the Lord; for his _____ endureth for ever"?
   Love, Good, Mercy, Spirit
4. "In every thing give thanks: for this is the _____ of God."
   Power, Will, Gratitude, Travail
5. A sacrifice of thanksgiving is most meaningful when it is . . . ?
   Sincere, Often, At your own will, Extravagant
6. Where was Jonah when he prayed with the voice of thanksgiving?
   Fish's belly, Aboard ship, In the wilderness, Mountaintop

ANSWERS:
1. Neither (Feminine name meaning thankfulness)
2. Unthankful people (2 Timothy 3:1–2)
3. Mercy (Psalms 106:1)
4. Will (1 Thessalonians 5:18)
5. At your own will (Leviticus 22:29)
6. Fish's belly (Jonah 2:1, 9)

Score Correct: _____ Date: _____ Name: _____
Study Notes: _____
_____
_____

Quiz 200: Christmas Flavored

1. Is the book of Advent in the Old Testament, New Testament, or neither?
2. Who did Jesus's mother, Mary, stay with while she was expecting?
   Joanna, Dinah, Jael, Elisabeth
3. In what type of clothes did Mary wrap the newborn Jesus?
   Admonishing, Resurrecting, Swaddling, Castling
4. Jesus was born in Bethlehem of . . . ?
   Nazarene, Jerusalem, Judaea, Capernaum
5. The wise men came to see the baby Jesus from which direction?
   North, South, East, West
6. What was the number of wise men that came to see the baby Jesus?
   Unspecified, 2, 3, 4

ANSWERS:

1. Neither (Coming of our Savior, and on the calendar, includes four Sabbaths before Christmas)
2. Elisabeth (Luke 1:36, 56)
3. Swaddling (Luke 2:7)
4. Judaea (Matthew 2:1)
5. East (Matthew 2:1–2)
6. Unspecified (Matthew 2:1–12)

Score Correct: _____ Date: _____ Name: _____
Study Notes: _____
_____
_____

Quiz 201: Easter Flavored

1. Is the book of Eostre in the Old Testament, New Testament, or neither?
2. On watching Jesus's arrest and trial, what disciple claimed three times he didn't know the Lord?
   Judas, James, John, Peter
3. What does Pilate suggest be done to Jesus, that He be chastised and . . . ?
   Hung, Stoned, Crucified, Released
4. Who "platted" (plaited) the crown of thorns that Jesus wore?
   Herod, Soldiers, Pontius Pilate, Priests
5. When Mary came upon the risen Jesus, whom did He ask her to inform?
   Brethren, Priests, No One, Villagers
6. According to the Apostle Paul, higher than what number saw the risen Christ at one time?
   100, 300, 500, 1000

ANSWERS:

1. Neither (Originally the name for Spring Equinox celebrations)
2. Peter (Matthew 26:69–75)
3. Released (Luke 23:3–4, 14–17)
4. Soldiers (John 19:2)
5. Brethren (John 20:16–17)
6. 500 (1 Corinthians 15:6)

Score Correct: _____ Date: _____ Name: _____

Study Notes: _____

_____

_____

Jesus's ascension into Heaven
Courtesy of: clipart.christiansunite.com

Acknowledgments

Whenever there is a roll call of ones who made this work possible, there are always ones who are inadvertently left out. I apologize for that and will always cherish their hospitality, wise counsel, and genuine friendship. But to the ones listed and to any left out, I can only reciprocate but never repay. However, I do sincerely thank certain persons and resources whose unsung contributions to my work were very specific.

Lord God Almighty: The continued inspiration in my life
The Holy Bible: King James Version utilized throughout my research
Rita Rosenkranz: My literary agent and business partner, New York City
Caroline Russomanno: Skyhorse Publishing (Good Books) editor on project, New York City
Clipart.ChristiansUnite.com: Illustrations utilized throughout

Proofreaders:
Carolyn Allen, Spartanburg, South Carolina
Colleen Casey, Spartanburg, South Carolina
Ben Chumley, Spartanburg, South Carolina
Steve Duncan, Spartanburg, South Carolina
Laura Edwards, Spartanburg, South Carolina
Joyce Finkle, Spartanburg, South Carolina
Toni and Jeff Hesla, Spartanburg, South Carolina
Philip W. Holman, PharmD, Gaffney, South Carolina
Deb Jolly, Spartanburg, South Carolina
Dot Jolly, Spartanburg, South Carolina

Kelli C. Lanford, Boiling Springs, South Carolina
Don P. Morgan Sr., Pauline, South Carolina
Buddy Pittillo, Spartanburg, South Carolina
Lynnette Quinn, Lanford (Station), South Carolina
John D. Robeson, PhD, Cedar Rapids, Iowa
Frank Sanders, Spartanburg, South Carolina
Brad Tate, Union, South Carolina
Deno Trakas, PhD, Spartanburg, South Carolina
Marianna Shaver Weathers, Woodruff, South Carolina
Jeannie Wilson, Enoree, South Carolina

And to any/all others inadvertently omitted, my sincere thanks.

Index

For index entries referencing an image, "f" has been added following the page number.

confession to, 5
Cornelius encountering, 15
delivering apostles from
　Jerusalem prison, 78
fought against Satan, 69
Gideon encountering an, 7
as guardian of Eden, 18
rescued Lot, 99
Animal(s), 12, 37
Anna, 71, 99, 139
Annas, father-in-law of
　Caiaphas, 41
Antichrist spirit, 30
Apostles
　on not to stone the, 118
　preaching the Gospel, 105f
　releasing from prison, 117
"Apple tree", 188
Aquila and Priscilla, relationship
　of, 57
Ararat mountains, 124
Ararat, 94
Arimathaea, 113
Ark of the Covenant, 8, 35, 37,
　39, 110
Armoni, 171
Ashkelon, 69
Asiel, 101
Asmodeus, 205
Assyria, 137, 201
Athaliah, 124
Athaliah, ruler of Judah, 162
Azariah, 149

B
Baal, prophets of, 70
Baalis, 90
Babel, Tower of, 20, 21f
Bad things, God and stopping, 7
Balaam, 5, 27, 32
Baptism, of Jesus, 1, 53, 136

Bar-jesus, 74
Barabbas, 127
Barad, 174
Barak, son of Abinoam, 72
Bariah, 138
Barnabas, 160
　biblical name of, 1
　name of, 15
　place deserted by Mark, 46
Bartholomew, 186
Bathsheba, 165
Bathsheba, King Solomon's
　mother, 82
Beerlahairoi well, 149
Beersheba, altar in, 83
Behemoth, 15
Bela, 119
Believers, as part of priesthood,
　58
Belteshazzar, as name for
　Nebuchadnezzar, 88
Benhadad, 38, 81
Benjamin, 116, 159
Benjamin tribe, 70
Benjamites, 115
Bernice, 104
Bethany, 70
Bethel, 47, 142, 198
Bethesda pool, 41
Bethshan, 89
Bible
　books beginning with letter
　　"D," 192
　books beginning with letter
　　"H," 125
　books beginning with letter
　　"L," 199
　books beginning with letter
　　G, 57
　books starting with letter
　　"R," 167

command of army in, 188
first five books of, 12
men in the name of Dodo in, 18
natural disaster in the, 173
seasoning mentioned in, 45
serpent in, 170
word "eternity" in, 24
Biblical times, large unit of
money or weight in, 50
Blind man, healing of, 59
Boaz, 39
Bochim, 173
Book of "Remembrance", 190
Bread loaves, to feed five
thousand, 121
Brides, command of, 22
Brooks, names referring to, 104
Burning bush, 99, 129, 188

C
Caesarea Philippi, 136
Caiaphas, father-in-law of, 41
Cain, 120, 185
descendant of, 135
exile to the land of Nod, 75
name of first child, 156
son of, 80
as tiller of the ground, 85
wife of, 123
Caleb, descendant of, 114
Cana, Jesus in, 79
Candace, as queen of Ethiopia,
117
Capernaum, 4, 10
Caves, names of, 94
Centurion, 87
Chariots lost, in Red Sea, 5
Charity, as gift of prophecies to
believers, 79
Chebar, 131
Cheirut, 207

Cherubim, 180
Children of God, peacemakers
as, 96
Christ
on the cross, 187
people placed faith in, 169
readiness for coming for
judgment, 127
Chronicles, 110, 145, 195
Church, 14, 17
Cities, destroyed by brimstone
and fire, 26
Claudius, 53
Concubines, 7
Constellation Orion, 2
Corinth, 158
Corinthians 1, 10, 62, 113, 122,
207
Cormorant, 48
Cornelius
encountering an angel, 15
as Roman soldier led to
Christ, 48
Creatures, in the vision of
prophet Joel, 47
Crete, 58

D
Daberath, 62
Damaris, 193
Damascus, 65, 111, 199
Daniel, 7, 33, 97, 100
dream of, 157
name for Nebuchadnezzar, 88
vision during king Cyrus, 114
Darius, 36, 92, 97, 103, 201
David, 68, 118, 150, 197
Absalom son of, 77
adulterous affair of, 16
after slaying Goliath, 32, 35
age at death, 35

longest, 29
Lord as strength and shield
in, 74
number of psalms in the book
of, 18
on referring to enemies, 54
shortest, 67
Pulpit, 55, 56

Q

Quartus, 197
Queen Sheba, 125, 126f

R

Rachel, 179, 183, 197
jealousy of sister's fertility, 16
stealing of images from her
father, 49
Rahab, 30, 95, 144
Rama, 81
Reba, 157
Rehoboam, king, 151
Reuben, as son of Jacob, 26, 38
Reuel, 56
Revelation, 44, 49, 52, 58, 83,
87, 104, 113, 119, 142, 151,
160, 170, 194
Righteousness, law of, 186
River Jordan, 1, 34
River Nile, 141
Romans, 1, 149, 159, 171, 174,
207
Rufus, 166
Ruth, 117, 169
marriage to Boaz, 70, 98
mother-in-law of, 155

S

Sadducees, 176
Safety, in putting trust in the
Lord, 32

Salmon, 95, 155
Salome, 30
Samaria, 38, 56, 110
Samaritan parable, Good, 37
Samson, 127, 161, 193
cutting hair of, 50
Delilah and betrayal of, 20
father of, 34
gates of Gaza destruction,
168f
imprisonment of, 13
as political enemy of
Philistine, 98
strength of, 79
women involved with, 167
Samuel, 71, 96, 97, 129
adulterous affair of, 16
anointment of David, 123
birth place of, 112
book of, 22, 107
growing up serving the Lord,
59
Jesse in, 5
mother of, 88, 102
son of Hannah and Elkanah,
125
Sapphira, name of mate, 163
Sarah, 125, 133
burial place of, 138
Egyptian handmaid, 13
lying to God, 3
mentioned (at death), 119
wife of Abraham, 13
Sarai, 85, 124, 148
Sardis, 178
Satan, 201, 202
Saul, 149, 153, 154, 200, 205
"evil spirit," 112
asking woman as medium, 38
body nailed to a wall with his
sons, 89

Sword of the spirit, 86
Syrian soldiers, Elisha and, 14

T
Tabitha
  apostle that raised, 36
  as pet name, 17
Tahpenes, Egyptian queen in the
  bible, 164
Talent, as large unit of money or
  weight, 50
Tarshish, 123
Tarsus, 132
Tekoa, 33, 113
Ten Commandments, 206
Thaddaeus, 175
"The Prince of Peace", Jesus as,
  28
Thessalonians, 72, 160, 188
Thomas, other name of, 1
Thoughts of peace, and not of
  evil, 4
Thyatira, 133
  purple goods from, 40
Timothy, 11, 148, 156
Titus, 73
Tower of Babel, 20, 21f
Trinity, 60
Twenty four rules for restitution,
  117
Tyre, 24

U
Ur, 88
Uzzah, Ark of the Covenant
  and, 8
Uzzi, 11
Uzziah
  age as king of Jerusalem, 77,
  120

reigned fifty-two year as king
  of Jerusalem, 134

V
Valentine, 204
Vashti, 20
Vision
  of angels going up into
    Heaven, 15
  of barley cake, 77
  to contract Simon Peter, 81
  of Daniel during king Cyrus,
    114
  of dry bones, prophet famous
    for, 40
  Ezkiel in, 78
  of heaven, Peter, 74
  of Jacob, 79
  of John, 103
  measuring Jerusalem, 65
  of Nebuchadnezzar, 7
  of Pharaoh, 14
  of the prophet Joel, 47
  of Wickedness women, 18

W
Wilderness, 9, 29, 43, 80, 156,
  157, 186
Wise/wisdom, 66170
Woolites, 128
Worship in churches, on first day
  of the week, 10

Y
Year of Jubilee, 73

Z
Zacchaeus, in Jericho, 88
Zachariah and Elisabeth, name
  of child, 103
Zaphnath, 23

Author **Wilson Casey's** Other Skyhorse Publishing Books

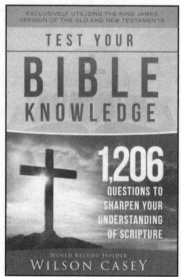

For a complete list of the **50+** works by **Wilson Casey,**
please visit his Amazon Author Page!